# What Are Your Odds at the Blackjack Table?

- When should you buy "insurance"?
- When do you split and resplit?
- Doubledown?
- Draw or stand?
- What is the best basic strategy?
- Is counting really necessary?
- Playing strategies for—hard hands, soft hands, multiple-deck games, single-deck games and no-hole card games.
- Why is blackjack the *only* casino game which can be mastered through skill?

# A Book on Casino Blackjack

## C. Ionescu Tulcea

**Inside tip:** This book is the best guide to the game of Blackjack (Twenty-One) and winning strategies for all major casinos here and abroad.

# A BOOK ON CASINO BLACK-JACK

C. Ionescu Tulcea

PUBLISHED BY POCKET BOOKS NEW YORK

POCKET BOOKS, a division of Simon & Schuster, Inc.
1230 Avenue of the Americas, New York, N.Y. 10020

Copyright © 1982 by Van Nostrand Reinhold Company Inc.

Published by arrangement with Van Nostrand Reinhold Company Inc.
Library of Congress Catalog Card Number: 81-10483

ISBN: 0-671-47397-2

First Pocket Books printing November, 1983

10 9 8 7 6 5 4 3 2 1

POCKET and colophon are registered trademarks
of Simon & Schuster, Inc.

Printed in the U.S.A.

# Preface

In this book we discuss the game of blackjack (or twenty one) as played in Nevada, Atlantic City, England and other parts of the world. This book is written for the general public. No special knowledge is required for the reading of this book.

The material we present is gathered in five chapters. In Chapter 1 we describe the game, the basic rules offered by the casinos and most of the variations of these rules the player may encounter.

In Chapter 2 we explain the basic strategy. This strategy can be mastered quickly and is optimal for the player who does not keep track of the cards. While the basic strategy is not a winning strategy, the player who follows it, exactly as it is given here, has a much better chance of a winning streak than the player who bases his decisions on "intuition and the usual common sense." The basic strategy depends on the rules under which the game is played. For example, one should not use the same strategy whether or not the dealer draws to soft 17.

In Chapters 3 and 4 we describe, in detail, two new winning strategies, the main-count system and the 99-count system. Betting and playing strategies, depending on the count, are given. The bet variation, in the betting tables in this book, is from 1 to 12. While in certain situations this betting range must be reduced (or the betting strategy modified) the player must realize that in actual games, particularly in multiple-deck games, he cannot win without varying his bet. Of the two systems mentioned above, the main-count system is the simpler one. Nevertheless, this system is excellent for both betting and playing decisions.

In Chapter 5 we discuss betting procedures, describe playing conditions in various casinos and indicate how the player may compute the running index (which, for various reasons, we prefer to true counts).

We close by noticing that it was E. O. Thorp who first published winning blackjack strategies (most of his work appeared in the first edition of his famous book, *Beat the Dealer*) and that among the most important research on blackjack is the work of P. A. Griffin.

We take this opportunity to express our thanks to the collegues and friends who helped in the preparation of the manuscript of this book, especially to Ralph Boas and to Henry Cejtin, Paul Shick and Denis White.

C. IONESCU TULCEA
Mathematics Department, NU
Evanston, Illinois 60201

# Contents

## 3  WINNING STRATEGIES IN BLACKJACK. THE MAIN-COUNT SYSTEM / 52

## 4  THE 99-COUNT SYSTEM AND THE ADJUSTED COUNT SYSTEM / 81

# A BOOK ON
# CASINO
# BLACK-
# JACK

# 1
# The Blackjack Game

*Blackjack,* or *twenty one,* is a game played with cards between one or several players and a dealer who represents the house. Roughly speaking, the goal of each of the players is to obtain a hand having a value greater than that of the dealer's hand, but without exceeding 21.

Blackjack is one of the two most popular casino games. The other is the dice game of craps. In blackjack, one must make strategic decisions. These decisions affect the outcome of the game and hence give the players the feeling that, to a certain extent, they control the game. Also, blackjack is, at present, the only casino game in which the player can obtain an advantage over the house by skill.

The reader should not conclude from the above remarks that the decisions one has to make are obvious and that most players make the right ones. Unfortunately, very few players make correct betting and playing decisions. As a colleague of mine said sometime ago, the game of blackjack is such that when one makes strategic decisions according to "intuition and common sense" many of his decisions will be completely wrong.

While anybody can learn how to play winning blackjack, only very few will make the necessary effort. One cannot learn the game by reading a book on blackjack during a flight to Las Vegas or to London. There are very few skillful players. Nevertheless, even casino managements overestimate their number by a wide margin.

Most blackjack is played in casinos in the continental United States. Nevertheless, the game is played in Europe, particularly England, the Caribbean, Canada, and many other parts of the world. At present, the popularity of the game as well as the number of casinos offering it is growing.

In the rest of this chapter we shall indicate how the game is played, describe the options a player has and make various observations. The material is useful to both the beginner and the knowledgeable player. Winning strategies will be given in Chapters 3 and 4. A short historical note concerning blackjack systems is also given in Chapter 3.

## THE VALUE OF A HAND (HARD AND SOFT HANDS)

To describe the game we must know what we mean by the *value of a hand* (or of a group of cards). The difference between *hard hands* and *soft hands* is particularly important.

The jacks, queens, and kings are called *face cards*. These cards are always counted 10. The aces are counted 1.* The other cards are counted as their face values indicate. For example,

are counted, respectively, 3, 6, and 10.

The card suits (clubs, diamonds, hearts and spades) have no significance in the game of blackjack.

*Whenever we say that a card is a ten, we mean that the card is one of the cards counted* 10. For example, a jack is a ten, a queen is a ten, etc.

An ace will usually be designated by the letter A.

---

*Traditionally, aces are counted "1 or 11." This is probably the reason for the confusion concerning soft hands.

The hand

consists of a 2, a ten, and a 6. *The value of this hand* is, by definition, 18 (observe that 18 = 2 + 10 + 6). *The value of the hand:*

is 25. *The value of the hand*

is 7.

Observe that the hands we considered until now did not contain aces. It is somewhat more difficult to introduce the value of a hand containing aces. To define the value of such a hand we proceed as follows:  First, as we have already indicated, each ace in our hand is counted 1.  The *number* we obtain is called the *hard value of the hand*.

For example, the hard value of

**Fig. 1a**

is 16 (observe that 16 = 10 + 5 + 1).  The hard value of

**Fig. 1b**

is 8 (observe that 8 = 1 + 1 + 6).  The hard value of

**Fig. 1c**

is 22.

*The value of a hand containing aces is defined to be equal to its hard value, if the hard value is 12 or more. If the hard value is 11 or less, then the value of the hand is*

hard value + 10.

For example, the value of the hand in Fig. 1a is 16, since the hard value of this hand is 16, and 16 is more than 12. The value of the hand in Fig. 1b is 18. In fact, the hard value of this hand is 8, whence its value is

$$8 + 10 = 18.$$

The value of the hand in Fig. 1c is 22.

*A hand is said to be soft if it contains aces and if its hard value is 11 or less. All other hands, whether or not they contain aces, are hard.*

Therefore, a hand which does not contain aces is always hard. A hand containing aces is hard only when its hard value is 12 or more. Observe that the value of a hard hand containing aces coincides with its hard value.

Notice that if you add a ten to a soft hand, the value of the new hand cannot exceed 21. Hence, you cannot "bust" by drawing to a soft hand. We should also notice that the value of a soft hand does not change when you add a ten.

Here are more examples: The hand

is soft and has the value of 18 (the hard value of this hand is 8). The hand

is also soft and the value 21 (the hard value of this hand is 11). The hands

and

are both hard and have the value 17.

Additional examples are given in the table below. The first column indicates the composition of the hand. The second indicates whether the hand is hard or soft and the last column shows the given value of the hand:

| | | |
|---|---|---|
| A, 7 | soft | 18 |
| A, 7, 10 | hard | 18 |
| A, 2 | soft | 13 |
| A, 2, jack | hard | 13 |
| A, A | soft | 12 |
| A, A, A | soft | 13 |
| A, A, A, 8 | soft | 21 |
| A, 9 | soft | 20 |
| A, 9, 5 | hard | 15 |
| 2, 4, 3 | hard | 9 |
| 2, 4, 3, A | soft | 20 |
| 2, 4, A, 2 | soft | 19 |
| 2, 4, jack, 2 | hard | 18 |
| 2, A, 2, 6, A, 3, 4 | hard | 19 |
| 2, A, jack, queen | hard | 23 |
| A, A, jack, jack | hard | 22 |

A *stiff* is a hard hand having a value of

12, 13, 14, 15, or 16.

The 9s, tens and aces will be called *high cards*. The cards counted

2, 3, 4, 5, 6, or 7

will be called *low cards*.

## THE GAME

The game of blackjack is played at a table like the one in Fig. 2. There are six or seven chairs for the players and, on the table, six or seven *betting areas*. The game can be played with one to seven players.

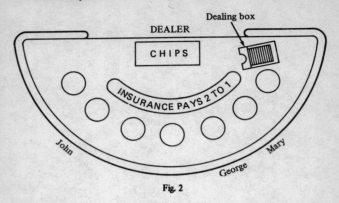

Fig. 2

Nowadays, most blackjack games are multiple-deck games.\* *In this book we always assume that the considered games are four-deck games, unless we say explicitly the contrary.* Nevertheless, most of the strategies we describe can be used, with very little error, for all multiple-deck games. Variations and customs are discussed in the next section.

The game proceeds as follows: Assume that there are three players at the table, Mary, George, and Jack. Each player has some *chips*, bought from the dealer, or from the casino cashier. Each player makes a bet by placing one or more chips in the corresponding betting area. Sometimes, currency is used for bets, particularly for large ones.

The dealer shuffles the pack of cards and offers it to one of the players for a cut. The cut is usually performed by inserting a plastic card in the pack and by interchanging the two parts determined by the card. The cut must be made: If the players at the table do not want to, the dealer must make it. A plastic card (the joker) is placed about 60–70 cards from the end of the pack.† The first card is dealt and placed – face down – in a small box to the right of the dealer.\*\*

The dealer gives a card to Mary, a card to George, a card to Jack, and a card to himself (this last card is dealt face up). Then again he gives a card to Mary, a card to George, a card to Jack and finally a

---

\*When more than two decks are used, the cards are dealt from a *shoe* (a *shoe* is a *dealing box*).

†The joker is often placed much higher. The higher the joker is inserted, the worse off the (skillful) player.

\*\*The players must place their bets before this card is dealt.

card to himself (this time the dealer's card is dealt face down). Hence, each one of the players has two cards. The dealer also has two cards, one face up and one face down (*this last card is the dealer's hole card*).

It is extremely important for the casino that the players do not see the dealer's hole card. If the players knew what this card was, they could quickly win huge amounts of money by using a judicious playing strategy. On the other hand, there is no disadvantage for a player if his cards are seen by the other players or by the dealer. In fact, in many blackjack games the player's cards are dealt face up. In this case, the players are not supposed to touch the cards. In fact, one of the reasons for this policy is to make cheating harder. There are known cases when players marked (or tried to mark) the cards during play, for their benefit or for the benefit of a confederate. It is not hard to imagine the huge advantage gained when only a few of the tens are marked.

A game in which the cards are dealt face up is advantageous for the skillful player, since he can see more cards before he decides what to do. Also, it is easier to follow the cards when they are dealt face up. When the cards are dealt face down, a player may glimpse a card of another player, and then, by the time that card is turned face up, may forget what it was.

A hand consisting of two cards, one of which is an ace and a ten, is a *blackjack* (or a *natural*). Clearly, a blackjack is a soft hand of value 21. Only *the first two cards dealt to the player, or to the dealer, may form a blackjack.* For instance, if you split two tens (see the section on splitting) and get an ace on one of them, you have a hand of value 21, but this hand is not a blackjack — it is not paid as a blackjack.

When the dealer's up card is a ten or an ace, he must inspect immediately his hole card. If the value of his hand is 21, *then he turns his hole card up.*

If the dealer's hand is a blackjack, he collects the bets of all the players who do not have blackjack. These players lose their bets. The players who have blackjack, if there are any, tie the dealer. For instance, if both Jack and the dealer have blackjack, Jack's cards will be removed, but his bet will be left in its place. Jack tied — or pushed — the dealer. He has neither gained nor lost anything.

If George has a blackjack and the dealer does not, then (no matter what the dealer's cards are) George wins an amount equal to *one-and-a-half* times his bet. Hence, if George bet $100, he wins $150. Hence, he collects in all, his initial bet included, $250.

Assume now that the dealer does not have blackjack. If Mary does not have a blackjack either, then she has the option of *standing* (not asking for additional cards) or *drawing* (asking for additional cards). Other options the player has, for example, *splitting, doubling down, insurance, surrender*, etc., will be discussed in the following sections.

If Mary does not like her hand, decides to draw, and signals so, the dealer will place one card in front of her initial hand (see Fig. 3).* If

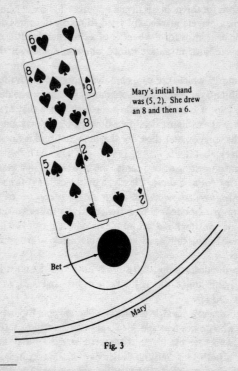

Mary's initial hand was (5, 2). She drew an 8 and then a 6.

Bet

Mary

**Fig. 3**

---

*Here we assume that the players cards are dealt face up. For the case when the cards are dealt face down, see the next section.

she is still not satisfied with the hand, she may ask for further cards, which will be dealt to her successively. To ask for a card, Mary either scratches the table with one of her hands or points towards the cards. To signal that no card is wanted, Mary positions her hand with the palm towards the dealer, as if to say "no more." In any case, if at any moment the value of her hand exceeds 21, she *busted* (she lost) and the dealer will collect her bet and remove her cards.

Once Mary has played her hand, it is George's turn and then Jack's turn, to play their hands.

If all the players at the table have busted, the dealer collects all the bets, removes all the cards on the table and starts dealing again (from left to right).

If some of the players at the table did not bust, the dealer turns up his hole card. If his hand has a value of 17 or more, he is required by the rules of the game to stand. If he has less than 17, the rules require that he draws until the value of his hand becomes at least 17. He must stand, as soon as he makes 17 or more. Obviously, the dealer may bust – exceed 21 – by drawing cards.

There is an *important exception* to the above rules. *In some casinos the dealer draws to soft* 17. The dealer may bust by doing so, for instance by drawing a 9 and then a 6, or a 5 and then a ten, etc. In any case, this rule increases in the long run, the house advantage, but only slightly.

Assume now that the dealer did not bust and that the value of his hand is 19. He compares his hand with the hands of the players at the table, who did not bust. For example, if George's hand has the value 20, then George wins. If he bet $25, he wins $25. If George has 18 (or less than 18) he loses his $25 bet. If George's hand has the value 19, then he *ties* (or *pushes*) the dealer. In this case he neither wins nor loses. The dealer will remove the cards, but will leave the player's bet on the table.

Once the settlement, corresponding to a round of play, is made, the game continues as indicated before.

In many casinos, players may simultaneously play as many hands as they wish, if there are enough adjacent free places at the table. In others, they may play at most three hands. Players who play more than one hand are generally required to place higher bets. In some casinos, the gambler who is alone at a table, must play at least two hands.

As we said above, in blackjack games offered in legal casinos, ties are not won by the dealer. Stay away from games in which the house takes the ties. In such games the player's disadvantage is overwhelming. *These games should be avoided even when they are offered in schools, at fairs, carnivals, etc.*

In the above description of the game we assumed that the dealer receives both cards from the beginning and that he immediately checks his hole card, when the up card is a ten or an ace. This manner of dealing, while the most prevalent at this time, is not universally adopted. In certain casinos in England, in the eastern United States, etc., the dealer's hole card* is dealt only after all the gamblers at the table played their hands. We shall refer to such games as *no hole-card games.* For various reasons, we shall divide this class of games into two groups. We observe first that in casinos where the dealer's hold card is dealt and checked from the beginning, when the up card is a ten or an ace, the player may split or double down only after it was determined that the dealer does not have blackjack. In *no hole-card games* the situation is different. If the player decides to split or double, he must do so before the dealer's hole card is dealt. *Under one set of rules, when the player splits or doubles down and the dealer ends with a blackjack, all the bets are lost.* This is unfavorable for the player. For example, assume that the player bets $25, that he receives two aces and that the dealer has an ace up. The player splits and receives a 9 on the first *ace and a queen on the second.*[†] The dealer gets a ten for his hole card, and hence ends with a blackjack. The player will lose now $50. Games played under the set of rules described here will be referred to as *no hole-card games of type I* (or as *no hole-card games English style*). *Under a second set of rules, only the initial bet is lost, when the player splits or doubles down and the dealer ends with a blackjack.* This set of rules represents only a manner of dealing the game. The final outcome is not affected in any way. Games played under this set of rules will be referred to as *no-hole-card games of type II.*

We observe that in no hole-card games the dealer cannot cheat the casino by signaling a confederate what his hole card is.

---

*We continue to refer to this card as hole-card, although, being dealt at the end of the round of play, the card is exposed immediately.
[†] Remember that only the first two cards dealt to the player may form a blackjack.

Unless we say explicitly the contrary, we assume that the dealer receives his hole card at the beginning of each round of play and that he checks this card immediately, when he has a ten or an ace up.

The house establishes a *minimum* and a *maximum* bet, for each table. In Nevada, the minimum bet is usually between $1 and $5 and the maximum bet between $500 and $3,000. There are of course many variations. In any case, one would have a hard time finding a plush casino where $1 bets can be made at a blackjack table. The minimum and the maximum bets allowed are indicated, almost always, on each table. In some places only selected players are allowed to bet the maximum limit. I have seen, recently, a list of names of such gamblers at a major Las Vegas strip casino. The persons to whom these casinos convey such "honors" are probably poor blackjack players.

## VARIATIONS AND CUSTOMS

As we have mentioned before, most blackjack games are dealt from multiple decks. There are, of course, exceptions. For example, in downtown Reno most of the games are dealt from a single deck.

Under the same rules, the advantage of the house increases when the number of decks, used in the game, increases. However, the dealer needs much more skill to cheat, when the cards are dealt from a shoe.

Games played with more than one deck were generally dealt from two decks or four decks. More recently a number of casinos started to use five or more decks and to insert the joker very high. Some casinos (particularly those in Atlantic City) even use eight-deck shoes. Whenever possible players should stay away from such games unless special favorable rules are offered. We often prefer to play in four-deck games (instead of one- or two-deck games), but we do not see any reason to accommodate the houses which introduced five or more deck games, and do not offer, at least, special favorable rules. For the readers who wonder why we prefer four-deck games we observe that such games are safer, *when the cards are shuffled well*. Whether or not the cards are really shuffled is often difficult to ascertain. We know very well what can be done with decks kept in hand. The mannerisms of the great majority of dealers is such that a person sitting at a blackjack table cannot say for certain whether the dealer peeked at the top card or whether he dealt a second.

In a single-deck game the dealer may shuffle the deck any time he wishes, even after dealing one hand only. In four-deck games the dealer will not shuffle before the joker is dealt. If the joker is encountered during a round of play, that round is usually completed and only then is the pack shuffled. Hence, in such games, the players know in advance when the shuffling will take place. This does not mean that there are no exceptions to the above rules. There are, but they seldom occur. Once, in a casino on the Las Vegas strip, the dealer shuffled in the middle of the shoe, when I insured a (10, 5) and then, since the dealer did not have blackjack, I surrendered the hand. That casino claims not to bother skillful players. Maybe, after all, they leave alone only the players who are skillful, but not those who are too skillful.

When the game is dealt from a single deck, the players' initial cards are dealt face down. In multiple-deck games, the cards are often dealt face up.

When the cards are dealt face down, the player should hold the cards as indicated in Fig. 4. To signal that a card is wanted, the player should *brush* the table, lightly, with the corner indicated by the arrow (see Fig. 4). The words *hit* or *card* may also be used, when requesting a card.

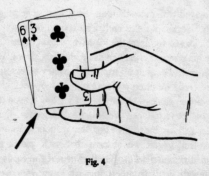

**Fig. 4**

If the player decides to stand, before or after asking for additional cards, the cards should be placed under the bet, as shown in Fig. 5. The player should try to do this with one hand, and without touching the bet.

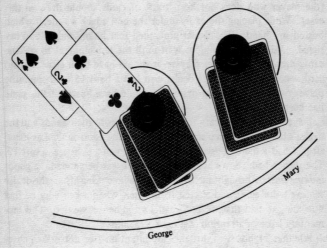

George

Mary

**Fig. 5**

As stated in the previous section, when the cards are dealt face up, to ask for a card, the player either *ratches* the table with one of the hands, or *points* toward the cards. To signal that no card is wanted, the player should position his hand with the palm towards the dealer, as if to say "no more" and wave the hand sideways.

Players should learn, before sitting at the table, how they should signal what they want to do. The dealer cannot read their minds. Generally, there are also other players at the table, and these players may not tolerate the delays caused by beginners who do not know what to do and who, in addition, stubbornly refuse to follow the dealer's instructions on how to signal "their decisions." These beginners should also understand that the dealer cannot establish special signals for every new player. I suggest that they read, at least, the first chapter of this book, and that they watch the game, for a few minutes, before sitting at a blackjack table.

The players should not give the dealer any opportunity to say that he misunderstood their signals.

One early morning at a casino in Las Vegas, I was dealt hard 15. The dealer had a 7 up. The strategy I was using required to stand (the player who does not keep track of cards should draw in this case). While placing the cards under the bet, a jack was dealt which busted my hand. The dealer pretended that he misunderstood my signal. Aside from having to wait until the last moment to see the cards drawn by the other players, it should have been clear that no card was asked. Since the dealer also had a hard 15 (and since the player on my left did not draw), he would have busted if the game had been dealt correctly.

Players should also learn to quickly count both their hands and the dealer's hand. Once, in a single-deck game in a casino on the Las Vegas strip, I had a hand consisting of an ace, a 2 and a 6, hence, a soft 19. The dealer had 18. While the settlement was being made, a *good-looking hostess* brought me a martini. While looking at her, the dealer removed the cards and started to shuffle. When asked why he had not paid, he said that we both had 18 and hence, we tied. This momentary lapse of attention cost me a $25 chip.

Whether or not such mistakes are intentional or not makes absolutely no difference for the player who loses the bet.

Also, watch out for "funny" dealers who collect immediately all the bets on the table, without even looking at the players hands, when they end with a 21 or 20.

In the next sections, of this chapter, we shall describe in detail the main options the player has in the game of blackjack.

## DOUBLING DOWN

Doubling down is one of the most important options the player may exercise in the game of blackjack. In many casinos, the player may double down after receiving the first two cards, *no matter what these cards are*.

We shall now explain how to exercise the option: Assume that after receiving the first two cards, Jack decides to double down.* He

---

*Here we assume that the player's cards are dealt *face up*.

will say "double down" (or "double") and will double his intial bet by adding an equal amount (placed to the left or right of the initial bet). He will be dealt óne, and only one, card (see Fig. 6). This hand now consists of three cards. *The settlement will be made by comparing the value of this hand with the value of the dealer's hand.*

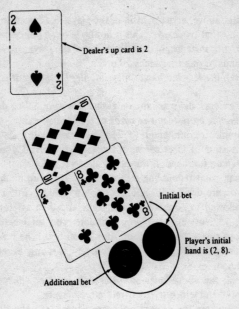

Dealer's up card is 2

Initial bet

Player's initial hand is (2, 8).

Additional bet

**Fig. 6**

The "double down ritual" is somewhat different when the cards are dealt *face down*. In this case the player says "double down," places his cards on the table, face up, and doubles the initial bet. Again, he will be dealt one, and only one card, face down.

In general, the dealer will understand that you intend to double down, when you double your bet, even if you do not say "double down." There are, however, cases when it is not clear whether the player wants to double, or to split (see the next section).

The player should not double on any hand of hard value 12 or more. Hard 11 is, in general, a very good hand for doubling down.

Since, for instance, a four-deck pack contains 64 tens, the player who doubles on 11 has a good chance of ending with a hand of value 21.

Judicious double-down decisions increase the player's chances. When the player should double down is indicated in the following chapters.

As we said above, in many casinos, the player is allowed to double down on any first two cards. This is not however, a policy universally adopted. For instance, in downtown Reno, the player may double only on hands having the values 10 or 11.

In general, *the less the player may double, the better it is for the house.*

It is *an exceptional case* when a casino allows doubling down *on hands containing more than two cards* or *redoubling.*

For example, if your hand is (3, 2) and you are dealt a 6, you have a hand consisting of *three cards,* of value 11. In general, you should double down on this hand, if the casino allows it.

To explain what redoubling means, assume that you double on 8 and that you are dealt a 3. You have now a hand of value 11. You might be allowed to double your bet again, and then ask for a card ("redouble"). Notice, that if you redouble, you total bet will be equal to four times the amount of your initial bet. The redoubling rule is favorable to the player. Unfortunately, it is only exceptionally encountered.

In general, the above rules are offered in casinos which are not doing too well and which try to attract more players.

In casinos where the dealer's hole card is dealt and checked from beginning, and when the up card is a ten or an ace, the player may double down only when the dealer does not have blackjack. In no hole-card games the player must double down before the dealer receives his hole card. In *no hole-card games of type I,* the player loses all the bets if the dealer ends with a blackjack. The correct doubling down strategy for such games is given in the following chapters. In *no hole-card games of type II* only the initial bet is lost when the dealer ends with a blackjack.

Doubling after splitting is an important option, favorable for the player. It is discussed in the next section.

## SPLITTING

When the first two cards have the *same count, the player has the option to split*. For example, the player may split the following hands:

In some casinos, the splitting of tens is somewhat restricted. The player cannot split a hand consisting of two different types of face cards (for instance, a king and a queen) or a hand consisting of a face card and ten which is not a face card. This rule is often encountered, for example, in the Reno–Tahoe area.

It is important to remember that if you split two tens and receive an ace on one of them, the hand so obtained is not a blackjack — and is not paid as a blackjack. The same holds if you split two aces and are dealt a ten on one of them. A hand is a blackjack only when the initial two cards are an ace and a ten.

We now explain how to exercise the option to split. Assume that George's hand consists of two 8s and that he decides to split.* He will say "split" and will double his inital bet by adding an equal amount (placed to the left or right of the initial bet). The 8s and the bets will be positioned as shown in Fig. 7. A card will be dealt on the 8 to the player's right. This hand will be then completed in the usual manner — the player may stand or draw additional cards (see also the end of this section). Only afterwards, cards will be dealt on the 8 to the player's left.

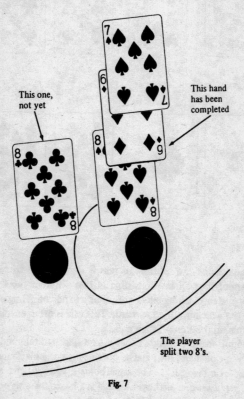

This one,
not yet

This hand
has been
completed

The player
split two 8's.

**Fig. 7**

---

*Incidentally, two 8s should almost always be split.

In general, by looking at your hand, the dealer will understand that you want to split, when you double your bet, even if you do not say "split." Nobody will double down on 16, or 14, etc., and nobody can split (4, 7), or (5, 4), etc. There are however cases when the situation is not so clear. For example, when the hand is (5, 5) or (4, 4). Two 5s should never be split. In any case, this does not mean that bad players do not split such hands. Sometimes, two 4s should be split.

Usually, the player is allowed to split more than once. For example, if George splits two 8s and is dealt another 8 on one of them, he may split again, if he desires so. In a majority of casinos, the player may split at most *three times* (hence, he may obtain at most four hands by splitting). In some casinos, there is no limit to the number of times the player may split. In others, the player may split only the initial hand.

There is an important difference in the case of hands consisting of two aces. Generally, the player who splits such a hand receives *one, and only one, card* on each one of the two aces. The player cannot split again or draw additional cards.

In casinos where the dealer's hole card is dealt and checked from the beginning, when the dealer's up card is a ten or an ace, the player may split only when the dealer does not have a blackjack. In no hole-card games the player must split, if he decides so, before the dealer receives his hole card. In *no hole-card of type I* the player loses all the bets if the dealer ends with a blackjack. The correct splitting strategy for such games is given in the following chapters. In *no hole-card games of type II* only the initial bet is lost when the dealer ends with a blackjack.

An important variation is when *the player may double down after splitting a hand*. For instance, assume that the dealer's up card is a 5 and that Jack's hand consists of two 7s. He splits, and receives a 4 on the 7 to his right. He has now a hand of value 11 on which he may double down, if the above rule variation is in effect.

*Doubling down after splitting is a favorable option for the player and should be exercised whenever possible.*

One should observe, that in certain cases, whether players should split, depends on whether they are allowed to double down after splitting. For instance, the player who does not keep track of cards, should split (3, 3) against a 2, if doubling down after splitting is allowed and should not split otherwise. Complete details will be given later.

In certain casinos (in England) the player is not allowed to split 4s, 5s, and tens. Interestingly enough, these rules are imposed "to protect the players."

### INSURANCE

In most casinos, the player has the option of placing an additional bet called *insurance,* when the dealer has an ace up.* This bet is placed on the table, in front of the main bet, in the area marked:

"Insurance pays 2 to 1"

The insurance bet can be at most half of the main bet. For example, if the player's main bet is $100, the insurance bet can be at most $50. In what follows we discuss only the case when the amount of the insurance bet is exactly half of the main bet.

*The player wins the insurance bet when the dealer has blackjack and loses otherwise.* In case of a win the payoff to the player is 2 to 1.

To clarify the meaning of the insurance bet, assume that John's main bet is $100, that the dealer has an ace up, and that, after looking at his hand, John places a $50 insurance bet. Two cases are possible:

1. *The dealer has blackjack.* If John does not have blackjack he loses his main $100 bet, but wins $100 with the insurance bet. In this case, he neither loses nor gains anything. If John has blackjack, he ties with the main bet and wins $100 with the insurance bet. Hence, he has a profit of $100.
2. *The dealer does not have blackjack.* In this case John loses his insurance bet. Afterward he must play his hand, which he might win, tie, or lose.

We notice that if John has blackjack and takes insurance, he will win an amount equal to his main bet, no matter what the dealer's

---

*The player who makes such bets is *taking insurance.*

hand is.* For this reason, many players insure immediately when they have blackjack and the dealer has an ace up. Nevertheless, easy calculations show that insurance should not be taken.

The players who do not keep track of cards and insure their blackjacks win less, in the long run, than those who do not insure.

Bad players insure when they have a good hand and do not insure when they have a bad hand. Obviously, they are influenced in their action by the usual meaning of the word "insurance."

*As a general rule, the players who do not follow the cards should not insure, no matter what their cards are.*

*The players who keep track of tens should insure if**:*

3 X the number of unseen tens $\geqslant$ the number of unseen cards. (1)

*Observe, however, that not all the cards which are dealt are necessarily seen.*

It follows from (1) that if, for instance, a gambler plays in a two-deck game and if 25 tens and a total of 74 cards remain unseen, he should insure, since

$$3 \times 25 = 75$$

and 75 is greater than 74. However, if only 24 tens remain among the unseen cards, he should not insure, since

$$3 \times 24 = 72$$

and 72 is less than 74.

As will be indicated later, the players who do not keep track of tens, but use various other count systems, should also insure in certain conditions. While these players will derive a profit from insurance, only those who follow the tens can *always* make correct insurance decisions.

When the cards are dealt face down, and you play more than one hand, you must finish playing your first hand (the one to your ex-

---

*Remember that the payoff to a player who has blackjack is 2 to 1 — unless the dealer has blackjack also.
**This is one of the many basic results, in blackjack, obtained by E. O. Thorp.

treme right) before you are allowed to look at the other hands. There is, however, an exception to this rule. When the dealer has an ace up you may check all your hands before deciding whether or not to take insurance. Of course, once you checked your hands, you should either insure all of them or none. Remember that the decision to insure depends on the composition of the deck, or decks, used in play, and not on your hands. If you keep track of cards, look at all your hands even if you know that you will not take insurance. This way you will see more cards before you decide what to do next.

Many players, even good players who know when to insure, do not understand how the insurance bets affect the player's capital.

Assume that a player, Ralph, has two stacks of chips. One consisting of *white* chips and one consisting of *blue* chips. Ralph uses the white chips only for main bets and the blue chips only for insurance bets. The rules governing the insurance bets show that the stack of white chips varies independently of that of blue chips. If Ralph does not keep track of cards, and always insures, we can prove mathematically that the stack of blue chips will decrease in the long run. It follows therefore that the insurance bet is disadvantageous for the player who does not keep track of cards.

As we have already said, the insurance option can be exercised in most casinos, but not all. Also, in some casinos, particularly overseas, players are allowed to insure only when they have blackjack. In certain no hole-card games the players may insure only after completing their hand. If they bust, they cannot insure anymore. This is unfavorable to the player.

*Insurance is an important and favorable option for the player who keeps track of cards.*

## SURRENDER

An interesting option called *surrender* is offered in a few casinos and is favorable to the skillful player. There are many "forms" of surrender. In the United States, the most common one, is as follows: *No matter what the dealer's up card is, the player may surrender the first two cards for half of the initial bet. The player may surrender only if the dealer does not have blackjack.*

For example, assume that George made a $100 bet, he receives (9, 7), and the dealer has a ten up (but does not have blackjack). In this case, George may surrender his hand. If he decides to exercise this option, the dealer will remove $50 from his bet and leave the rest for George.

Incidentally, the players who do not keep track of cards should surrender (9, 7) when the dealer has a ten up. A complete set of rules is given in Chapter 2.

Many players do not know when to surrender. Other players do not like to surrender.

A few years ago, I was playing blackjack at the Dunes, in Las Vegas. I was receiving bad hands and I was surrendering many of them. "You are giving your money away without a fight," said the dealer, a pleasant young man. I smiled and answered: "Probably I am looking for an easy way out." I did not say, of course, that if I would have fought, I would have given even more money away.

Consider, for example, the case of (9, 7) against a dealer's ten. This is a *losing hand*, no matter what one does. As we indicated above, the players who do not keep track of cards should surrender this hand. We can prove mathematically that the players who do not surrender, lose more in the long run.

Assume that the cards are dealt *face down*. To surrender, the player must turn the cards face up and say "surrender." The player must make certain that the dealer understands what he wants to do.

Special care should be taken when the cards are dealt *face up*. To surrender, in this case, the player should say "surrender" (loud enough). *The player should keep his hands still and away from the cards.* Any movement of the hands might be interpreted by the dealer as "hit" or "stand."

Sometime ago, I was playing at the Riviera, in Las Vegas, in a four-deck game. The cards were dealt face up. I was sitting to the dealer's right and I was dealt (10, 5). The dealer had a 10 up. I said "surrender," but somehow the dealer misunderstood my signal and dealt a jack. I am certain that the mistake was unintentional. The dealer had a 6 under the ten. Hence, the jack would have busted her. The next card in the shoe was a 3, giving her a total of 19. All this happened very quickly, before I could say anything. I protested, and so did one other player at the table, the pit boss was called to arbitrate.

Graciously, he instructed the dealer to consider her hand a bust, and to pay everybody at the table.

In any case, try to avoid misunderstandings. They are not always solved in such a gentlemanly manner as at the Riviera.

A variant of the surrender option, described above, allows the player to surrender the first two cards only when the dealer has an ace or a ten up.

Another variant is the so called *early surrender*. It is offered mainly in the case of *no hole-card games*. *Under this rule the player may surrender before the dealer checks (or receives) his hole card*. When the dealer has an ace up, he has a probability of little less than 1/3, of ending with a blackjack. It is obvious therefore, that when early surrender is allowed, the player must surrender much more often. A complete strategy for early surrender is given in Chapter 2.\*

*Early surrender is very advantageous for skillful players.*

---

\*One other variant, encountered mainly in casinos in Asia, allows the player to surrender — under certain conditions — hands consisting of more than two cards.

# 2
# The Basic Strategy

In the first chapter we have described the rules of the blackjack game. We must differentiate, between the rules of the game, which tell what the player can or cannot do, and the strategy which should be adopted.

For instance, assume that you have two aces and the dealer has a ten up. By the rules of the game you may split or not, as you wish. But what is the best play in this case? If you do not keep track of the cards already dealt, then you should split. However, if you keep track of cards, the decision might be different. For example, if you know that the remaining cards are mostly 3s, 4s, and 5s, then you should not split. In fact, if you split, you will probably end with two soft hands of value 16 or less, and the dealer will beat both of them (remember that in most casinos you cannot draw further, when you split two aces).

By keeping track of the cards dealt from the pack used in the game, and by skillful play, the player can gain an advantage over the casino. *Blackjack is the only game for which winning strategies can be devised.* Such strategies will be given in the next chapters.

In this chapter we describe the *basic strategy* (also called the *zero-memory strategy*). The basic strategy is not a winning strategy. However, in a certain sense, it is at the basis of all winning strategies.

Of course, the ambitious player will not be satisfied with the basic strategy and will study a winning method. In any case, we should observe, that the basic strategy player has a much better chance of a "winning streak" than the bad player who bases his decisions on "hunches."

The basic strategy tells the player what the optimal playing decisions are, when these decisions are determined by the dealer's up card and by the player's hand. These decisions depend also on the rules under which the games are played.

In four-deck games played under *basic rules,* the player has a slight disadvantage of about 0.5%. In a one-deck game, and under the same rules, the player plays, for practical purposes, even with the house.

*By basic rules we mean that the dealer stands on soft 17 and that in addition to the options of drawing and standing the player may:*

> *insure;*
>
> *split and "resplit three times" (hence, the player may obtain four hands, at most, by splitting;*
>
> *double down on any first two cards.*

For various reasons, we listed the insurance option among the basic rules, although, strictly speaking, this option is of no interest to the basic strategy player.

When the player may double down after splitting pairs, his expectation, expressed in percent, increases by about 0.14.

When the player is not allowed to double down on soft hands, his expectation decreases by about 0.09.

When the player is not allowed to double down on hard 9, his expectation decreases by about 0.09.

When the player may double down only on hard 10 and hard 11, his expectation decreases by about 0.19.

When the player may double down only on hard 11, his expectation decreases by about 0.7 (this bad rule is encountered, for instance, in casinos in Puerto Rico).

When the dealer draws to soft 17, the player's expectation decreases by about 0.2.

In no hole-card games of type I (no hole-card games English style) the player's expectation decreases by about 0.13.

The basic strategy given in this section is essentially the same as that given first by R. Baldwin, W. Cantey, H. Maisel, and J. McDermott in their famous papers (see Refs. 4 and 5) and then by J. Braun, R. Epstein, E. O. Thorp, and A. N. Wilson. The research by J. Braun deserves special mention (see for instance, Ref. 7). Various related results are given in Refs. 20, 23, and 50.

In the following sections we describe the basic strategy for multiple deck games and single deck games.

*In the rest of this book we assume, unless stated explicitly the contrary, that the games are played under basic rules.*

We assume therefore that the dealer stands on soft 17. Nevertheless, games in which the dealer draws on soft 17, are also discussed.

Possible options, which are not offered in casinos, or are offered only in exceptional cases, might not be discussed in this chapter.

The basic strategy player should exercise the *playing options* in the following order:

split and resplit;
double down;
draw or stand.

When offered, the surrender option or the early surrender option should be exercised first. Of course, the playing options should be exercised according to the recommendations in the following sections.

## THE BASIC STRATEGY FOR MULTIPLE-DECK GAMES

We shall give now the basic strategy for four-deck games. The same strategy should be used for all multiple-deck games. Also, except for a few cases we mention below, the same strategy should be used, whether or not the dealer draws on soft 17.

### Drawing and Standing (Hard hands)

The decisions to draw and stand are the most important a player makes in the game of blackjack.

With a hard hand of value 11 or less (that is 11, 10, 9, . . .) the player should *draw*, independently of the dealer's up card.

With a hand of value 17 or more (that is 17, 18, . . .) the player should *stand*, independently of the dealer's up card.

With a hand of value 12, 13, 14, 15, or 16, the player should proceed as indicated in Table 1. This table is read as follows: We determine the *block* located to the *right* of the number representing the value of the player's hand and under the number representing the dealer's up card. If this block is *shaded*, the player *should stand*. If the block is *white*, the player *should draw*.

## Table 1.

These numbers represent the
dealer's up card

| | 2 | 3 | 4 | 5 | 6 | 7 | 8 | 9 | 10 | A |
|---|---|---|---|---|---|---|---|---|---|---|
| **17** | | | | | | | | | | |
| **16** | | | | | | | | | | |
| **15** | | | | | | | | | | |
| **14** | | | | | | | | | | |
| **13** | | | | | | | | | | |
| **12** | | | | | | | | | | |

These numbers represent the
value of the player's hand

For example, assume that the player's hand has the value 14 and the dealer has a 7 up. The block to the right of 14 and under 7 is *white*. Hence, in this case the player should *draw*.

Assume that the player's hand has the value 13 and the dealer has a 4 up. The block to the right of 13 and under 4 is *shaded*. Hence, in this case, the player should *stand*.

Assume now that the player's hand has the value 12 and the dealer has a 3 up. The block to the right of 12 and under 3 is *white*. Hence, in this case the player should *draw*.

Some players hesitate to draw when their hand has "high" values. The table shows that the correct strategy is to *draw until you have at least* 17, when the dealer's up card is a 7, 8, 9, 10 or A.

Certain other players have the tendency not to draw when their hand has *more than two cards. This is a major mistake.* For instance, assume that the player has a hand of value 13 and the dealer has a 7 up. By the basic strategy, the player should draw. Assume that a 2 is dealt. The value of the player's hand is now 15. The player should draw again. Assume that an ace is dealt. The value of the player's hand is now 16. By the basic strategy the player should draw again. It is obvious that this is the last time the player will draw, during this round of play. In fact, once the next card is dealt the player will either bust or end with a total between 17 and 21.

The decision to draw on 16 against a ten is a close one. In fact it is closer than those of drawing or standing against 7, 8, 9 or A.

A more detailed analysis shows that in certain cases the decision to draw or stand depends not only on the value of the hand but also on its composition. However, these cases are marginal and will not be discussed here.

### Drawing and Standing (Soft Hands)

The player's strategy for drawing and standing with *soft hands*, is even simpler than that for hard hands.

When the dealer's up card is a

$$2, 3, 4, 5, 6, 7 \text{ or } 8$$

*the player should draw to any soft hand of value 17 or less and stand otherwise.* Hence, the player should stand on soft hands of value 18 or more.

When the dealer's up card is

$$9, \text{ten or A}$$

*the player should draw to any soft hand of value 18 or less and stand otherwise.* Hence, the player should stand on soft hands of value 19 or more.

For instance, the player should stand on (A, 7) if the dealer's up card is 8. However, the player should draw on (A, 7) against a 9, ten or A.

Of course, many players hesitate to draw to soft 18. Such a good hand! In any case, computations show that it is a mistake to stand on soft 18 when the dealer's up card is 9, ten or A.

The following two examples help explain how to handle soft hands.

1. Assume the dealer has an 8 up and the player, (A, 6). Hence, the player has soft 17. The player should draw in this case (remember that with hard 17 the player should stand). Assume he receives a ten. The player has now a hand consisting of A, 6, and ten. This is a hard hand of value 17. The player should now stand.

2. Assume the dealer has a 5 up and the player soft 16. Many players stand in this case. Computations show that this is a mistake. As we said above, the player must draw to soft 16. In fact, the player holding (A, 5) against a 5 should double down (see the section on doubling down with soft hands).

*Observe that the only way a player holding soft 16 can fail to lose is for the dealer to bust.* If he draws, he might get a 2, 3, or 4. In this case, he will substantially improve his hand. If he draws any other card he will not worsen his position against the dealer. If he draws an ace, he has soft 17, and therefore should draw again.

### Doubling Down (Hard Hands)

With a *hard hand* the player should consider doubling only when the hand has one of the values 9, 10, or 11. When the player should double is indicated in Table 2.

### Table 2.

These numbers represent the
dealer's up card

|    | 2 | 3 | 4 | 5 | 6 | 7 | 8 | 9 | 10 | A |
|----|---|---|---|---|---|---|---|---|----|---|
| 11 |   |   |   |   |   |   |   |   |    | ▨ |
| 10 |   |   |   |   |   |   |   |   | ▨  | ▨ |
| 9  | ▨ |   |   |   |   | ▨ | ▨ | ▨ | ▨  | ▨ |
| 8  | ▨ | ▨ | ▨ | ▨ | ▨ | ▨ | ▨ | ▨ | ▨  | ▨ |

These numbers represent the
value of the player's hand

Table 2 should be read as follows: You determine the block located to the right of the number representing the value of your hand and under the number representing the dealer's up card. If the block is *white, you should double. If the block is shaded, you should not double.*

For example, assume that the player's hand is (4, 5) and the dealer has a 6 up. The value of the player's hand is 9. The block to the right of 9 and under 6 is white. Hence the player should double. If the player has the same hand and the dealer has 8 up, then the player should not double since the block to the right of 9 and under 8 is shaded.

*Notice that you always double with a hard hand having the value 11, except when the dealer has an ace up. You always double with a hand having the value 10, except when the dealer has a ten or an ace up.*

In the case of two-deck games the player should follow the above tables, except for the following cases:

Double on (6, 5) and (7, 4), when the dealer has an ace up.

Double on a hand of value 9, when the dealer has a 2 up.

When the dealer *draws to* soft 17, double on hard 11 against an ace.

### Doubling Down (Soft Hands)

With a *soft hand,* the player should consider doubling only when the hand held has a value of 13, 14, 15, 16, 17, or 18. When the player should double with such a hand is indicated in Table 3. This table should be read in the same way as Table 2, in the previous section.

Notice that with a soft hand you never double against 2, 7, 8, 9, 10, or A. You double against 3 only when you have *soft* 17 or *soft* 18.

### Table 3.

These numbers represent the
dealer's up card

| | 2 | 3 | 4 | 5 | 6 | 7 | 8 | 9 | 10 | A |
|---|---|---|---|---|---|---|---|---|---|---|
| 20 | | | | | | | | | | |
| 19 | | | | | | | | | | |
| 18 | | | | | | | | | | |
| 17 | | | | | | | | | | |
| 16 | | | | | | | | | | |
| 15 | | | | | | | | | | |
| 14 | | | | | | | | | | |
| 13 | | | | | | | | | | |

These numbers represent the
value of the player's hand

When the dealer *draws to soft* 17, double on (A, 8) against a dealer's 6 and on (A, 7) against a dealer's 2.

In many casinos, for example in downtown Reno, the player is not allowed to double on soft hands.

Restrictions on doubling are very unfavorable to the player. Such restrictions are common, for example, in downtown Reno.

### Splitting (When Doubling Down After Splitting Is Not Allowed)

In Table 4, we give the strategy for splitting pairs. Table 4 should be read as follows: Determine the block to the right of the numbers representing the player's pair and under the number representing the dealer's up card. If the block is *white*, split. *If the block is shaded, do not split.*

For instance, if you have two 9s and the dealer has a 7 up, you do not split since the block to the right of (9, 9) and under 7 is shaded.

**Table 4.**

These numbers represent the dealer's up card

| | 2 | 3 | 4 | 5 | 6 | 7 | 8 | 9 | 10 | A |
|------|---|---|---|---|---|---|---|---|----|---|
| A, A | | | | | | | | | | |
| 10, 10 | ▓ | ▓ | ▓ | ▓ | ▓ | ▓ | ▓ | ▓ | ▓ | ▓ |
| 9, 9 | | | | | | ▓ | | | ▓ | ▓ |
| 8, 8 | | | | | | | | | | |
| 7, 7 | | | | | | | ▓ | ▓ | ▓ | ▓ |
| 6, 6 | ▓ | | | | | ▓ | ▓ | ▓ | ▓ | ▓ |
| 5, 5 | ▓ | ▓ | ▓ | ▓ | ▓ | ▓ | ▓ | ▓ | ▓ | ▓ |
| 4, 4 | ▓ | ▓ | ▓ | ▓ | ▓ | ▓ | ▓ | ▓ | ▓ | ▓ |
| 3, 3 | ▓ | | | | | | ▓ | ▓ | ▓ | ▓ |
| 2, 2 | ▓ | | | | | | ▓ | ▓ | ▓ | ▓ |

These numbers represent the player's hand

If you have the same pair and the dealer has, for example, 9 up, you split, since the block to the right of (9, 9) and under 9 is white.

Observe that you should split (8, 8)* and (A, A), no matter what the dealer's up card is. Observe also that you never split (4, 4), (5, 5) and (10, 10).

If you have (5, 5), the value of your hand is 10; you never split this hand. If the dealer's up card is a

$$2, 3, 4, 5, 6, 7, 8 \text{ or } 9$$

you should double down. In two-deck games split (6, 6) against a 2.

### Splitting (When Doubling Down After Splitting Is Allowed

As we already wrote in the first chapter, the option of doubling down after splitting is favorable to the skillful player. *When this option is offered, the player should split more often.* The strategy for splitting pairs, under these conditions, is given in Table 5. This table should be read in the same way as Table 4.

#### Table 5.

These numbers represent the dealer's up card

These numbers represent the player's hand

| | 2 | 3 | 4 | 5 | 6 | 7 | 8 | 9 | 10 | A |
|---|---|---|---|---|---|---|---|---|---|---|
| A, A | | | | | | | | | | |
| 10, 10 | ▓ | ▓ | ▓ | ▓ | ▓ | ▓ | ▓ | ▓ | ▓ | ▓ |
| 9, 9 | | | | | | ▓ | | | ▓ | ▓ |
| 8, 8 | | | | | | | | | | |
| 7, 7 | | | | | | | ▓ | ▓ | ▓ | ▓ |
| 6, 6 | | | | | | ▓ | ▓ | ▓ | ▓ | ▓ |
| 5, 5 | ▓ | ▓ | ▓ | ▓ | ▓ | ▓ | ▓ | ▓ | ▓ | ▓ |
| 4, 4 | ▓ | ▓ | | | | ▓ | ▓ | ▓ | ▓ | ▓ |
| 3, 3 | | | | | | | ▓ | ▓ | ▓ | ▓ |
| 2, 2 | | | | | | | ▓ | ▓ | ▓ | ▓ |

---

*When early surrender is offered, the player should surrender (8, 8) against a ten or an ace, instead of splitting.

Observe that you never split (5, 5) or (10, 10). When the option of doubling down after splitting is offered, you split (4, 4) if the dealer's up card is a 5 or 6. Dealers and various players often criticize such playing decisions, particularly if you lose one or more of the hands you obtained by splitting. Do not listen to them and do not try to explain why you split. But remember, when doubling down after splitting is allowed, the correct decision is to split (4, 4) against a 5 or 6.

### Insurance

Strictly speaking, the basic strategy player should not insure. This is true if we assume that the player's decisions depend only on the following three cards: the dealer's ace and his first two cards. Nevertheless, if for example, the player plays two or more hands or sees additional cards before he makes his decisions, the situation is somewhat different.

As stated in the previous chapter, only the players who keep track of tens can make *always* correct insurance decisions. These players should insure if:

$$3 \times \text{ the number of unseen tens} \geq \text{the number of unseen cards (2)}$$

Observe that (2) is equivalent to saying that the number of unseen tens divided by the number of unseen cards is $\geq 1/3$.

From (2) we deduce several immediate rules:

*One-deck games:* Never take insurance on the first round of play, if you have seen only your two cards and the dealer's up card. In fact, in this case you have seen 3 cards. Hence, 49 more remain in the deck. Since a complete single-deck contains 16 tens and

$$3 \times 16 = 48$$

the relation (2) does not hold.

If you play two hands and if there are no tens among your cars, then you should take insurance. In fact, in this case you have seen 5 cards. Hence, 47 remain to be dealt. Since

$$3 \times 16 = 48$$

the relation (2) holds.

Notice that the above remarks imply that if the dealer has an ace up and your hands are, for example, (3, 4) and (7, 9), you should take insurance. However, if your hands are (A, 10) and (A, 10) you should not take insurance. Surprised?

*Two-deck games:* On the first round, you should not take insurance, unless you have seen at least 8 cards and none of them is a ten.

*Four-deck games:* You should never take insurance on the first round. The same recommendation holds in a five-deck game, six-deck games, etc.

In four-deck games, the player who does not keep track of cards, and takes insurance, is at a 7.2% disadvantage as far as these bets are concerned. The player who insures blackjacks, is at a 7.8% disadvantage. The player who insures when he has two tens, is at a 9.2% disadvantage.

The conclusions are similar, no matter what the number of decks used in the game is. However, the corresponding percent disadvantages depend on the number of decks, and are slightly different.

We close this section with the following remarks:

Assume that Robert participates in a four-deck game, that he does not keep track of cards, but plays "perfect" basic strategy. His decisions depend on the dealer's up card and on the first two cards he receives. He bets one unit each time.

Now assume that, in spite of the recommendations of the basic strategy, Robert decides to take insurance each time the dealer has an ace up. On the average, the dealer will have an ace up about 8 times in every 100 hands (more precisely, he will have an ace up, about "7.69 times" in every 100 hands). Assume that Robert plays 100 hands per hour. Then, during an hour he will place as insurance bets a total of about 4 units. Since he has a 7.2% disadvantage, he will lose an additional 0.28 of a unit (7.2% of 4 is about 0.28). It follows that, if his unit is $100, he will lose, on the average, an additional $28 per hour. In 8 hours of play he will lose about $224 more by taking insurance.

### Surrender

This option should be exercised whenever possible. Unfortunately, however, only few casinos offer surrender.

When the option may be exercised *only after it was determined that the dealer does not have blackjack,* the player should surrender* the following hands:

hard 16 [with the exception of (8, 8)] against 9, ten, or ace;
hard 15 [with the exception of (7, 8)] against a ten.
The pair (8, 8) should be split.

When the casino offers *early surrender,* that is, when the players may surrender *before the dealer checks his hold card,* the option should be exercised much more often. The corresponding optimal strategy is given in Table 6. All the hands in this table are *hard.* Observe also that, in Table 6, the pairs (8, 8) are listed separately from the other hands of value 16.

### Table 6

These numbers represent the dealer's up card

| These numbers represent the player's hand | 9 | 10 | A |
|---|---|---|---|
| 17 | | | ▓ |
| 16 | ▓ | ▓ | ▓ |
| 8, 8 | ▓ | ▓ | ▓ |
| 15 | | ▓ | ▓ |
| 14 | | ▓ | ▓ |
| 13 | | | ▓ |
| 12 | | | ▓ |
| 7 | | | ▓ |
| 6 | | | ▓ |
| 5 | | | ▓ |

---

*In Ref. 23, second edition p. 178, it is recommended that several more hands be surrendered, against an ace, when the dealer draws to soft 17.

The players should not surrender any hands which are not listed in Table 6.

The table should be read as follows: You determine the block to the right of the number (or numbers) indicating the player's hand and under the dealer's up card. If the block is *shaded*, the player *should not surrender*. If the block is *white*, the player *should surrender*. For example, the player should surrender 12 against an ace but not against a 9 or a ten.

We have already observed that the *early surrender* option is very favorable for the player. When this option is offered — in addition to the basic rules — the basic strategy player plays, for practical purposes, even with the house.

We indicated in the first chapter, that many players and casino employees do not understand how the surrender rule can be favorable to the player. In a book which contains many "pearls of wisdom" concerning gambling games, the authors also comment on surrender. They say that surrendering a hand does not make any sense to them and that they would rather take their chances and play the hand. Fortunately, whether or not the surrender rule makes any sense to these authors — and to certain other players — does not make any difference in the conclusions given in this book. The strategy recommended in this section is not obtained by "polling." A basic strategy determined "democratically" would certainly look very funny.

### No Hole-Card Games

In no hole card games of type I the player:

> should not double on 11 against a ten or ace;
> should not split (8, 8) against a ten or ace;
> should not split (A, A) against an ace.

The rest of the decisions should be made according to the strategy already given in this section.

In *no hole card games of type II*, the player should use the strategy previously given in this section.

### THE BASIC STRATEGY FOR ONE-DECK GAMES

The basic strategy for one-deck games is similar to that described in the previous section. Except in a few cases, which are mentioned explicitly below, the player should use the strategy given here, whether or not the dealer draws on soft 17.

### Drawing and Standing (Hard Hands)

The player should follow the four-deck strategy, given in Table 1, when his decisions are based on the *value* of his hand and the dealer's up card.

When the player takes into account the composition of his hand, he should:

stand on (8, 4), and (7, 5) against a 3;
draw to (10, 2) against a 4;
draw to (10, 3) against a 2;
stand on (7, 7) against a ten (see the remarks on surrender);
stand on hands of value 16 consisting of *three or more cards,* when the dealer has a ten up, with the exception of:

| | |
|---|---|
| (6, 6, 4) | (6, 7, 3) |
| (6, 8, 2) | (6, 9, A) |
| (6, 6, 2, 2) | (6, 6, A, 3) |
| (6, 8, A, A) | (2, 2, 2, ten) |

We observe that when the player has a two card hand with a value of 12, against a dealer's 3, he draws only if his hand is of the form (10, 2) (see the section on splitting).

### Drawing and Standing (Soft Hands)

The player should follow the four-deck strategy with the following exception:

stand on soft 18 against an ace, if the dealer *stands on soft 17.*

When the dealer draws to soft 17, the player should draw to soft 18 against a dealer's ace. In most casinos in Reno the dealer draws to soft 17. Hence, in these places, the player should draw to soft 18 against an ace.

### Doubling Down (Hard Hands)

The player should follow the four-deck strategy, given in Table 2, with the following exceptions:

double down on (5, 3) and (4, 4) against a 5 or 6 (when doubling down after splitting is allowed the player should split (4, 4) against a 4, 5, or 6);
double down on 9 against a 2;
double down on 11 against an ace.

### Doubling Down (Soft Hands)

The player should follow the four-deck strategy, given in Table 3, with the following exceptions:

double down on (A, 2) and (A, 3) against a 4;
double down on (A, 6) against a 2.

double down on (A, 8) against a 6;
do not double down on (A, 7) against a 2.

### Splitting (When Doubling Down After Splitting Is Not Allowed)

The player should follow the four-deck strategy, given in Table 4, with the following exceptions:

split (2, 2) against a 3;
split (6, 6) against a 2.

### Splitting (When Doubling Down After Splitting Is Allowed)

The player should follow the four-deck strategy, given in Table 5, with the following exceptions:

split (4, 4) against a 4;
split (6, 6) against a 7;
split (3, 3) and (7, 7) against an 8.

### Insurance

The basic strategy player should never insure. Do not insure (A, 10) or (10, 10)!

Of course, here we assume that the player plays one hand only and bases his decisions on his two cards, and the dealer's up card. When these conditions are not satisfied, the conclusion might be different (see the remarks on insurance in the first chapter and in the previous section).

### Surrender*

The player should surrender:

hard 16 [with the exception of (8, 8)] against a ten;
(10, 6) against an ace;
hard 15 [with the exception of (7, 8)] against a ten;
(7, 7) against a ten.

## VARIOUS RULES

To facilitate reference, we shall describe here various sets of black-jack rules which are often encountered.† *Whenever we specify a set of rules we mention only those which are different from the basic ones.*

### Reno-Tahoe Rules

The *Reno–Tahoe* rules are the following:

*doubling down on soft hands is not allowed;*
*doubling down on hard hands of value 9 or less is not allowed;*
*the dealer draws to soft 17.*

These rules are encountered in the Reno–Tahoe area. When the game is played under these rules *the player should draw to soft 18 against an ace.*

Games played under these rules are generally single-deck games.

---

*We assume here that the player may surrender only after it was determined that the dealer does not have blackjack.

†The reader should not infer that the corresponding rules are used throughout or only in the locations suggested by their names.

**British Rules**

The *British rules* are the following:

> *the game is a no hole-card game of type I;*
> *doubling down is allowed only on hard hands of value 9, 10, or 11;*
> *splitting of 4s, 5s, and tens is not allowed;*
> *pairs can be split only once;*
> *doubling down after splitting is allowed;*
> *only blackjacks can be insured.*

These rules are encountered in casinos in Great Britain.

**Eastern Rules**

The *Eastern rules* are the following:

> *doubling down after splitting is allowed;*
> *early surrender is allowed;*
> *pairs can be split only once.*

The Eastern rules were offered in Atlantic City. In 1981 the early surrender option, which is very favorable to the player, was eliminated. The elimination of this option is obviously related to the legal pressures put on the casinos not to bar "counters." The result of these pressures was to transform a very favorable game for the player into an unfavorable one. It would have been better for the player if the rules and playing conditions had remained as they were when the Atlantic City casinos opened.

In four-deck games played under Reno-Tahoe rules the player's expectation is about −0.87%. In one-deck games played under the same rules the player's expectation is about −0.46%. In games played under British rules the player's expectation is about −0.63%. In games dealt under Eastern Rules the player's expectation is about +0.24%. The substantial increase in expectation is due, mainly, to the early surrender option. The basic strategy player, betting $25 per hand, will make about $6 per hour (assuming that he plays 100 hands per hour).

## CHEATING

When dealt from a hand-held pack of cards, blackjack is one of the games in which it is easiest to cheat. It makes little difference if the pack consists of a single deck or of two decks. Nevertheless, a person with small hands will find more difficulty in handling two decks. There are innumerable methods one can use to cheat the player. The main ones are *peeking, dealing seconds and stacking*.

The reader should not infer from the above remarks that most dealers cheat. Neither should he believe that cheating does not exist. Players also try, sometimes, to cheat the casinos.

Before proceeding further we want to observe that, contrary to the general belief, a very long sequence of losing hands is not proof of cheating by the house. Many long sequences of winning hands also occur. The player who gambles for a long time will witness the occurrence of many unlikely events. For instance, on checking my notes about blackjack, I see that about ten years ago I was playing in a four-deck game at Caesars Palace, in Las Vegas. After half an hour I was left alone at the table. The dealer shuffled the cards and started dealing anew. And then a strange thing happened. Of all the hands dealt from the next two shoes I tied two and won all the others. What occurred was an extremely unlikely event.

### Peeking and Dealing Seconds

In blackjack games, peeking is usually done by executing a *front-peek* or a *back-peek*. The front-peek and the back-peek are illustrated, respectively, in Figs. 7 and 8.

The top card is a 3. The bend of the top card is exaggerated.

**Fig. 7**

**The position of the top card is exaggerated.**

**Fig. 8**

To perform a *front-peek,* the left thumb* "pushes" the top card toward the middle finger, which is held firm. The top card is read at the corner indicated by the broken arrow (see Fig. 7). A variant of this method is to loosen, somewhat, the fingers on the right side of the deck so that the top card does not bend, at first. To read the top card, one pushes it "back" with the middle finger.

The front-peek can be executed easily when, as many dealers do, the deck is kept vertically up and close to the chest. I assume that the gamblers who play in such conditions must be in search of places to make donations. The front-peek can be performed when the cards are dealt "toward the left" and the right forearm is brought above the left hand. It can be executed when looking at the wrist watch (set on the back of the left hand), when pointing with the left hand toward the player, etc.

To perform a *back-peek,* the left thumb "pushes" the top card in the sense indicated by the arrow. The top card is read at the corner indicated by the broken arrow (see Fig. 8).

The back-peek can be easily performed when looking at the wrist watch, when pointing the left hand toward the player, when arranging the chips in the money box, when collecting the cards from the table, etc.

Just before dealing to themselves the second card, many dealers position the pack of cards almost upside down. This, of course, is an unnecessary movement. In any case, when the cards are so positioned it is easy to back-peek at the top card (see Fig. 9). This manner of

---

*Throughout this section we assume that the dealer is right-handed.

back-peeking is excellent. In certain blackjack games, the dealer's "up card" is dealt face down and is not exposed until his hole card is dealt. In this case, the dealer who decides to peek has an additional advantage. The players will want to know what the "up card" is and hence, they will be looking at that card and not his hands.

It is particularly easy to back-peek when the up card is a ten or an ace and, hence, one has to check the hole card.

A variant of the back-peek described above can be used to read more than one card.

Peeking, by itself, is of no use to the person who deals. Indeed, the dealer's strategy is strictly determined by the rules of the game. Therefore, when the game is dealt honestly, it makes no difference if the dealer knows what the top card is. Nevertheless, peeking combined with dealing seconds, form an unbeatable cheating method.

*Dealing seconds* means dealing the card under the top one. The drawing in Fig. 10 illustrates how this sleight-of-hand is performed. The left thumb moves the top card into the position shown in the figure. The upper right corner of the second card is then exposed.

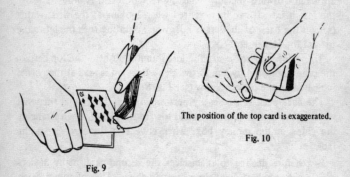

The position of the top card is exaggerated.

Fig. 10

Fig. 9

The *second* is "hit" with the thumb and pulled out, somewhat diagonally. If, for example, the upper side of the deck points toward north, the second is dealt toward northeast. A slight twisting movement of the left wrist helps make the sleight undetectable.

There are other methods of dealing seconds, but that described above is the classical one.

The following remarks explain how peeking and dealing seconds can be used in actual game. Assume for example, that the dealer has peeked and has seen that the top card is a 5. He can keep it there, by dealing seconds, until he has a 14, 15, or 16. He can make then 19, 20 or 21. By peeking and dealing seconds the dealer may also increase the probability of having a ten or an ace for his up card. One who uses marked cards does not need to peek. Nevertheless, in most cases, the use of marked cards is a crude method of cheating.

### Stacking

Stacking means setting all the cards, or only some of them, in a predetermined order. A "popular" method of stacking, disadvantageous for the player,* consists of arranging the cards in *low–high* or *high–low* order. This is, generally, done when the cards are removed from the table. It is not necessary that all the cards be arranged in low–high or high–low order. For the player to be at a disadvantage it is enough that the pack contains one or more such sequences.

When the pack contains several low–high or high–low sequences, the dealer has an additional advantage. For example, assume that he dealt a high card. Then, the probability that the next two cards are *low and high* is greater than normal. Hence, if he wants a low card he will deal the next one. If he wants a high card he will deal a second.

In relation to low–high and high–low stackings, the following experiment is of interest: A 52-card deck was divided into two parts, which were denoted L and H, respectively. In L we put all the low cards plus two 8s and in H, all the high cards plus two 8s. To facilitate the discussion below we shall refer to the cards in L as low cards and to those in H as high cards. The deck was set "at random" in *low–high* order. Hence, the first card was from L, the second from H, the third from L, the fourth from H, etc. A blackjack game was dealt to an imaginary player. The game was "honest" except for the stacking of the deck mentioned above, and was played under basic rules. No card was burnt. The game continued as long as the deck

---

*At least when he is alone at the table.

contained enough cards to complete the player's and the dealer's hands. The player bet one unit on each hand. The number of units, lost or won by the player was recorded.

The experiment was repeated 500 times. The same type of experiment was then repeated, 500 times, with decks set in *high–low* order. The results were the following:

In the case when the decks were set in low–high order the player lost a total of 1710 units.

In the case when the decks were set in high–low order the player lost a total of 1130 units.

Observe that in both cases the player's losses were very large. This is quite impressive since, in one-deck games played under basic rules the basic strategy player is not at a disadvantage. We conclude that the low–high and high–low stackings are devastating for the player.

One other method of stacking consists of inserting in the upper half of the pack of cards used in the game a proportion of high cards larger than normal. The pack so set is offered for a cut to a player, namely to "that player" who generally cuts in the middle. After the cut, the upper half becomes the lower half. Often, only the first half of the pack is dealt in an actual game, and then the cards are shuffled anew. In such a case the final effect is the same as that achieved by removing a number of high cards from the pack.

I will make here a few additional remarks concerning shuffling. No matter what the game is, I do not like to see one shuffling the cards with a "push in, pull out" movement and keeping the hands on the cards all the time. In this case it is nearly impossible to determine whether the cards "pulled out are different from those which were pushed in." Hence, it is difficult to ascertain that there has been any real shuffling. In blackjack it is, probably, better if one plays at a full table when the cards are not shuffled thoroughly.

### General Remarks

We have discussed above some of the technical aspects of peeking, dealing seconds, and stacking. As we have already said the reader should not infer that most casinos cheat. In fact, it is our opinion that the general policy of major casinos is to deal the games honestly.

Nevertheless, we prefer the blackjack games which are dealt from a shoe. With the exception of stacking, the main method of cheating in such games is by altering the composition of the pack of cards inside the shoe. If high cards are removed and low ones are added, the expectation of the house increases. Such an alteration is, however, material evidence in case of inspection. We do not believe that such altered shoes are used in major casinos.

To place our discussion in better perspective we want to make two remarks before proceeding further:

1. Peeking and dealing seconds cannot be detected when executed competently. Those who say otherwise do not know what they are talking about. Even a slow motion replay of a film taken with a high-speed camera will not reveal anything, unless the film is taken at "the right angle." Suspicious movements, yes, can be observed. Nevertheless, for various reasons, cheating cannot be inferred on the basis of such movements.

2. The best blackjack player cannot obtain more than a small advantage over the house. This player will end by being a loser if cheated *once or twice per hour* (see Refs. 19 and 23). In fact he will, probably, end by being a loser even if cheated only once every two hours, if the cheating takes place at the right time.

A skillful player will need many days of playing to recuperate what he may lose in one playing session against a skillful cheat.

The above remarks explain why an honest game is so essential for the skillful player. The average gambler will lose his money in any case if he plays long enough, no matter how the game is dealt.

The above remarks also explain why we prefer blackjack games dealt from a shoe. We do not like to place ourselves in a situation in which someone can cheat us, with a sleight-of-hand nobody can see. There is a major difference between participating in games in which cheating creates material evidence and participating in games in which cheating can be done by sleight-of-hand.

## Tables: The Basic Strategy for Multiple-deck Games

DRAW AND STAND (HARD HANDS)

|    | 2 | 3 | 4 | 5 | 6 | 7 | 8 | 9 | 10 | A |
|----|---|---|---|---|---|---|---|---|----|---|
| 17 |   |   |   |   |   |   |   |   |    |   |
| 16 |   |   |   |   |   |   |   |   |    |   |
| 15 |   |   |   |   |   |   |   |   |    |   |
| 14 |   |   |   |   |   |   |   |   |    |   |
| 13 |   |   |   |   |   |   |   |   |    |   |
| 12 |   |   |   |   |   |   |   |   |    |   |

Draw to (10, 2) against a 4.

DOUBLING DOWN (HARD HANDS)

|    | 2 | 3 | 4 | 5 | 6 | 7 | 8 | 9 | 10 | A |
|----|---|---|---|---|---|---|---|---|----|---|
| 11 |   |   |   |   |   |   |   |   |    |   |
| 10 |   |   |   |   |   |   |   |   |    |   |
| 9  |   |   |   |   |   |   |   |   |    |   |
| 8  |   |   |   |   |   |   |   |   |    |   |

In two-deck games, double on (6, 5) and (7, 4) against and ace and on 9 against a 2. When the dealer draws to soft 17 double on 11 against A.

DRAW AND STAND (SOFT HANDS)

When the dealer's up card is 2, 3, 4, 5, 6, 7, or 8, draw to any soft hand of value 17 or less and stand otherwise. When the dealer's up card is 9, ten, or A, draw to any soft hand of value 18 or less and stand otherwise.

DOUBLING DOWN (SOFT HANDS)

|    | 2 | 3 | 4 | 5 | 6 | 7 | 8 | 9 | 10 | A |
|----|---|---|---|---|---|---|---|---|----|---|
| 20 |   |   |   |   |   |   |   |   |    |   |
| 19 |   |   |   |   |   |   |   |   |    |   |
| 18 |   |   |   |   |   |   |   |   |    |   |
| 17 |   |   |   |   |   |   |   |   |    |   |
| 16 |   |   |   |   |   |   |   |   |    |   |
| 15 |   |   |   |   |   |   |   |   |    |   |
| 14 |   |   |   |   |   |   |   |   |    |   |
| 13 |   |   |   |   |   |   |   |   |    |   |

When the dealer draws to soft 17, double on (A, 8) against a 6.

## SPLITTING (WHEN DOUBLING DOWN AFTER SPLITTING IS NOT ALLOWED)

|        | 2 | 3 | 4 | 5 | 6 | 7 | 8 | 9 | 10 | A |
|--------|---|---|---|---|---|---|---|---|----|---|
| A, A   | ▓ | ▓ | ▓ | ▓ | ▓ | ▓ | ▓ | ▓ | ▓  | ▓ |
| 10, 10 |   |   |   |   |   |   |   |   |    |   |
| 9, 9   | ▓ | ▓ | ▓ | ▓ | ▓ |   | ▓ | ▓ |    |   |
| 8, 8   | ▓ | ▓ | ▓ | ▓ | ▓ | ▓ | ▓ | ▓ | ▓  | ▓ |
| 7, 7   | ▓ | ▓ | ▓ | ▓ | ▓ | ▓ |   |   |    |   |
| 6, 6   |   | ▓ | ▓ | ▓ | ▓ |   |   |   |    |   |
| 5, 5   |   |   |   |   |   |   |   |   |    |   |
| 4, 4   |   |   |   |   |   |   |   |   |    |   |
| 3, 3   |   |   | ▓ | ▓ | ▓ | ▓ |   |   |    |   |
| 2, 2   |   |   | ▓ | ▓ | ▓ | ▓ |   |   |    |   |

## SPLITTING (WHEN DOUBLING DOWN AFTER SPLITTING IS ALLOWED)

|        | 2 | 3 | 4 | 5 | 6 | 7 | 8 | 9 | 10 | A |
|--------|---|---|---|---|---|---|---|---|----|---|
| A, A   | ▓ | ▓ | ▓ | ▓ | ▓ | ▓ | ▓ | ▓ | ▓  | ▓ |
| 10, 10 |   |   |   |   |   |   |   |   |    |   |
| 9, 9   | ▓ | ▓ | ▓ | ▓ | ▓ |   | ▓ | ▓ |    |   |
| 8, 8   | ▓ | ▓ | ▓ | ▓ | ▓ | ▓ | ▓ | ▓ | ▓  | ▓ |
| 7, 7   | ▓ | ▓ | ▓ | ▓ | ▓ | ▓ |   |   |    |   |
| 6, 6   | ▓ | ▓ | ▓ | ▓ | ▓ |   |   |   |    |   |
| 5, 5   |   |   |   |   |   |   |   |   |    |   |
| 4, 4   |   |   |   | ▓ | ▓ |   |   |   |    |   |
| 3, 3   | ▓ | ▓ | ▓ | ▓ | ▓ | ▓ |   |   |    |   |
| 2, 2   | ▓ | ▓ | ▓ | ▓ | ▓ | ▓ |   |   |    |   |

## SURRENDER

Surrender hard 16 [with the exception of (8, 8)] against a 9, ten and ace.
Surrender hard 15 [with the exception of (7, 8)] against a ten.

## EARLY SURRENDER

|      | 9 | 10 | A |
|------|---|----|---|
| 17   |   |    |   |
| 16   | ▓ | ▓  | ▓ |
| 8, 8 |   |    | ▓ |
| 15   |   | ▓  | ▓ |
| 14   |   |    | ▓ |
| 13   |   | ▓  | ▓ |
| 12   |   |    | ▓ |
| 7    |   |    | ▓ |
| 6    | ▓ | ▓  | ▓ |
| 5    | ▓ | ▓  | ▓ |

**NO HOLE CARD GAMES (THE DEALER CHECKS HIS HOLD CARD AFTER YOU DOUBLED OR SPLIT AND COLLECTS ALL THE BETS IF HE HAS A BLACKJACK)**

Do not double down on 11 against a ten or an ace. Do not split (8, 8) against a ten or an ace. Do not split (A, A) against an ace.

# 3
# Winning Strategies in Blackjack
# The Main-Count System

In the previous chapter we described in detail the blackjack basic strategy. As we have already indicated, in four-deck games played under basic rules, the house has only a very small advantage over the basic strategy player. Moreover, single-deck games and even multiple-deck games in which additional favorable rules (for example, early surrender) are offered, are, for practical purpose, fair games. We recall also that the basic strategy player makes his decisions on the basis of the information furnished by the two cards forming his hand and the dealer's up card.

The above remarks suggest that if the player bases the betting and playing decisions on more information than that the basic strategy requires, he might obtain an advantage over the house. Indeed this is the case: Winning strategies can be devised for blackjack games. The supplementary information mentioned above is obtained by keeping track, one way or another, of the cards dealt from the pack used in the game. Of course, the player who could remember exactly the number of cards of each denomination which were seen and who could also make the necessary calculations would play optimally. Probably nobody is able to accomplish such feats.

For this reason, various ways of deriving *enough* information, if not complete, from the cards which were seen were invented. The usual methods are as follows: With each card a number (a weight) is associated. The numbers associated with the cards of the same denomination are identical. The numbers corresponding to the cards dealt and seen are added. The total, or better, the "normalized total," is used to derive information about the composition of the set of unseen cards. The information so obtained is used for making betting and playing decisions. The "normalized total" mentioned above tells the player not only when he has the advantage, but also gives an approximate measure of this advantage. The numbers (the weights) associated with the cards constitute a *point count.** The strategies based on the information given by a point count form a *point count system.*

Of course, the information obtained using a point count is not as complete as that we would obtain if we could keep track of each and every card. In any case, if the point count is adequate, the information it furnishes is substantial. The best players can obtain, by such methods, a 1%, 1.5% or even more global advantage. The advantage depends, of course, of how well the information is used, how good the point count is and how favorable the rules of the game are. In relation to the percent advantages mentioned above we observe that in the game of craps the house has about 1.4% advantage as far as the pass line bets are concerned. We also observe that if one plays with a 1% advantage and if one places on the table, during one hour, bets totaling $3,000, one will gain about $30. Since, in blackjack, one plays about 100 hands per hour, it is not hard to bet this amount. If the player gambles 8 hours per day, for a month, he will make about $7,200. Of course, if the bets are increased, the gain will be greater.

This chapter contains a discussion of the *main-count system.* This is a powerful method of play. The main-count is excellent for making both betting and playing decisions and does not require *corrections* for aces or other cards. This is very important since most players find either impossible or at least extremely hard to *correct* the count they use. We also observe that certain types of *corrections* are quite useless if one does not have a good estimation of the number of unseen cards. The main-count is better for making betting decisions than all published *one-parameter counts* which assign the value zero to the ace. In fact, no other count is better than the main-count for making both betting and playing decisions.

In recent years, it appears that authors of blackjack literature have put less emphasis on betting strategies. Reasons for this can be de-

---

*Instead of *point count* we shall often say, simply, *count.*

duced from certain remarks we make in the first section on betting in this chapter. Nevertheless, one cannot win in the usual multiple-deck games without increasing the amount of the bet in favorable situations. In this chapter we discuss in detail various betting strategies related to the main-count. More on betting will be said in Chapter 5.

## HISTORICAL NOTE CONCERNING WINNING STRATEGIES

The first published winning strategies were the *five-count* and the *ten-count*, both invented by E. O. Thorp. In Ref. 43, and particularly in his book *Beat the dealer*, (Ref. 44) he thoroughly studied these strategies. Many of his results, ideas, and methods were fundamental and created the basis for future research on the game of blackjack.

There were, of course, pre-Thorp players who could beat blackjack by skill. One of the most interesting exploits is that of a scientist and two associates who beat *multiple-deck games* in Cuba in 1958 (see Ref. 41, p. 66). The methods of play of these early winners are not known precisely. Although some of them were keeping track of tens and aces, most early strategies were approximate and were based on empirical observations.

Among the researchers working before or about the same time as E. O. Thorp* we mention R. Epstein and A. N. Wilson, the inventor of the *Wilson point count*.

We must also mention here the *machine* invented by R. Bamford, of the Jet Propulsion Laboratory (Pasadena, California), in 1960. On the basis of certain information, transmitted by the player, the machine recommended betting and playing strategies. It is interesting to observe that although these strategies were not optimal, the expectation obtained by employing the machine was higher than the expectations given by any of the modern "memory systems."

Soon after the publication of *Beat the dealer*, at the 1963 *Fall Joint Computer Conference*, held in Las Vegas, H. Dubner introduced a ± system (the High–low system). The system was studied in detail by J. Braun; it is presented in final form in his book (see Ref. 7). In addition to the work related to this system and that mentioned in the

---

*The research related to the basic strategy is mentioned in the introduction to Chapter 2.

introduction to Chapter 2, J. Braun did substantial other work on blackjack. Some of it is described in Ref. 6.

Among other blackjack systems, we mention here the Revere point count system, (Ref. 38), the 1973 Revere advanced point count system, (Ref. 39), the Gordon ± system, (Ref. 13), the Einstein–Humble system (advertised as the Hi-opt I), (Refs. 12 and 27), the Hi-opt II, (Ref. 13), the Griffin systems, (Ref. 13), the Complex count and the Adjusted count systems (Refs. 19 and 20), the Halves system (Ref. 51), and the Union system (Ref. 48). Important variants of the ten-count system are given in Refs. 2, 36, and 40.

In our opinion the most important theoretical research on blackjack, done in recent years, is that of P. Griffin (Refs. 21, 22 and 23).

## THE MAIN-COUNT SYSTEM**

The main-count is defined by the following table:

| 2 | 3 | 4 | 5 | 6 | 7 | 8 | 9 | 10 | A |
|----|----|----|----|----|----|----|----|----|----|
| +1 | +1 | +2 | +2 | +2 | +1 | 0 | 0 | -2 | -1 |

On the first line of this table we list the cards, and under each card, the value associated with it. The numbers associated with the cards are called *weights*. The weight of a 2 is +1, the weight of a ten is -2, the weight of an ace is -1,* etc.

We shall now introduce the *running count*. Afterwards, we shall introduce the *running index (normalized running count)*. In an actual game we estimate the composition of the set of unseen cards using the running count, or better, using the running index.

*Example.* – Assume that the game is dealt from a four-deck shoe. Assume that the first card we see is a 3. Since with a 3 we have associated the number +1 we say that, at this moment, the *running count* is

$$+1.$$

---

*The number $-1$ is read *minus one*. The number $-2$ is read *minus two*.

**The main-count was discussed, independently, by A. Snyder in his *Blackjack Forum* (September 1981) and in subsequent publications. A preprint containing the main parts of this chapter was prepared in February 1981.

Assume that the next card we see is a 7. Since with a 7 we have associated, again, the number +1, we add +1 to the previous running count (which is +1) and obtain for the next running count

$$+2.$$

Assume that the third card we see is a 5. Since with a 5 we have associated the number +2, the *running count* is now

$$+4.$$

If the fourth card we see, is again a 5, the *running count* becomes

$$+6 (+6 = +4 + 2).$$

Assume that the fifth card is a king. Since a king is a ten, and since with such a card we have associated the number –2, we add to +6 the number –2 (that is we subtract from 6 the number 2*) and obtain for the *running count*, at this moment of play, the number

$$+4.$$

Hence, the cards we have seen are

$$3, 7, 5, 5, king$$

---

*The numbers +1, +2, +3, +4, ... are called positive numbers (the symbols +1, +2, +3, +4, ..., respectively, 1, 2, 3, 4, ... mean the same thing). The numbers ..., –4, –3, –2, –1 are called negative numbers.

Whenever we say that, for instance, to the number +7 we *add* the number –4, we mean that we subtract 4 from 7. Hence +7 plus –4 equals +3 (in symbols, +7 + (–4) = +3).

There is a little difficulty here for those not familiar with negative numbers, since sometimes we have to add, for instance to +4 the number –7. In this case we obtain –3, that is

$$+4 + (-7) = (\text{to what?!}) - 3$$

The following examples will clarify the handling of negative numbers:

$$+4 + 3 = +7 \qquad +4 + 3 + 3 = +10$$
$$+1 + (-1) = 0 \qquad +2 + (-2) + 2 = +2$$
$$-7 + 4 + 3 = 0 \qquad -1 + (-1) + (-2) = -4$$
$$-2 + (-3) = -5 \qquad (-2) + (-3) + (-4) = -9$$
$$+1 + (-3) + (-3) + 5 + (-1) + (-6) = -7$$

and the corresponding *running count* is

$$+1 + 1 + 2 + 2 + (-2) = +4.$$

*Example.* — Assume that the game is dealt from a two-deck pack, and that the first six cards we have seen are

$$3, \text{queen}, 4, 8, 5, 10.$$

The corresponding *running count* is

$$+1 + (-2) + 2 + 0 + 2 + (-2) = +1.$$

*Example.* — Assume that the first four cards we have seen are

$$\text{jack, jack, queen, king.}$$

The corresponding *running count* is

$$(-2) + (-2) + (-2) + (-2) = -8.$$

If the next card we see is an ace, the *running count* becomes

$$-8 + (-1) = -9.$$

However, if instead of an ace the card would have been a jack, the *running count* would have become

$$-8 + (-2) = -10.$$

In an actual blackjack game, we must start to follow the cards, as soon as the pack is shuffled and the dealer begins to deal. As we already wrote, not all the cards which are dealt in the game, are necessarily seen. Obviously, when we determine the *running count*, or the *running index*, we take into account only the cards we can see. The more cards we see, the better it is. In fact, *we should try to see every card which is dealt.* Otherwise, the running counts and running indices we compute will be inaccurate. If, for whatever reason, you cannot see "many" of the cards which are dealt, then leave the game immediately.

It is quite easy to see that when there is an *excess of high cards* in the deck or decks used in the play then *the situation is, in general, favorable to the player.* Some of the reasons why the situation is favorable to the player, when there is an *excess of high cards* are the following: There is a better chance, in such a case, that a blackjack is dealt. The player and the dealer have the same chance to have a blackjack. However, if the dealer has a blackjack and the player does not, then the player loses the bet. But if the player has a black-jack and the dealer does not, then the player wins an amount equal to *one-and-a-half times the bet.* The dealer and the player also have the same chance to receive a *stiff,* for instance a hand of value 16. The dealer *has to draw* to such a hand while the player has the option to stand. Hence, if there is an excess of high cards in the deck, there is a greater chance that the dealer will bust. There is also a better chance to form a good hand when you double down on hard hands when there is an excess of high cards. Conversely, when there is an excess of low cards in the deck the situation is, in general, favorable for the house.

Since we have associated positive numbers with 2s, 3s, 4s, 5s, 6s, and 7s and negative numbers with tens and aces, it is obvious that, *in general:*

When the *running count* is a large positive number, there is an excess of high cards among the unseen cards.

When the *running count* is a small negative number,* there is an excess of low cards among the unseen cards.

In fact, if the *running count* is positive and large, we had to add many positive numbers to obtain it. Hence, many of the 2s, 3s, 4s, 5s, 6s, and 7s had to be removed from the pack used in the game, and hence, there must be an excess of high cards among those unseen.

Conversely, if the *running count* is negative and small, we had to add many negative numbers to obtain it. Hence, many of the tens

---

*If $a$ and $b$ are two of the numbers

$$\ldots, -10, \ldots, -3, -2, -1, 0, +1, +2, +3, \ldots, +10, \ldots$$

then $a$ is smaller than $b$ if $a$ is to the left of $b$. For instance $-10$ is smaller than $-5$, since $-10$ is to the left of $-5$.

and aces had to be removed from the pack, and hence, there must be in general an excess of low cards among the unseen ones.

From the above remarks we deduce that when the running count is large enough, the player has the advantage. In general, the player's expectation increases when the running count increases.

The strategy corresponding to the main-count is based, in fact, on the above observations. The same is true for the strategies corresponding to other point counts.

Once the *running count* has been determined, the next step is to introduce the *running index*. This is:

$$\frac{\text{running count} \times 100}{\text{number of unseen cards}} \qquad (3)$$

The running index increases when the running count increases and decreases when the running count decreases.

*Example.* — Assume that the game is played with a two-deck pack, and that the cards

$$A, 2, 6, 3, 3, \text{king}$$

were dealt and seen. Since a two-deck pack contains 104 cards, 99 remain unseen. The *running count* is

$$-1+1+2+1+1+(-2) = +2$$

and the *running index*

$$\frac{+2 \times 100}{99} = \frac{200}{99} = \text{about } 2.$$

If the game were played with four decks, and the same cards were dealt and seen, the *running index* would be

$$\frac{+2 \times 100}{203} = \frac{200}{203} = \text{about } 1$$

*We observe that the running count does not depend on the number of decks used in the game. It depends only on the cards dealt from the pack. The running index depends on the number of unseen cards, and hence, on the number of decks used in the blackjack game.*

The running count and the running indices in the above examples were computed on the basis of the main-count. *The calculations are similar when a different point count is used.*

The running index gives a better evaluation of the composition of the set of unseen cards, than does the running count. This is why the main betting and playing strategies in this volume are given using running indices. We observe, however, that it is often difficult to compute the running index. During actual play, this index should be determined using one of the methods described in Chapter 5.

## THE BETTING STRATEGY

As we have already written, to win in multiple-deck games, the player *must* increase the amount of his bet in favorable situations. Otherwise, he will waste time and money.

We have definitely observed that a player can learn quite quickly and easily how to vary the bet according to the count. Yet, the same player will usually have difficulties in varying correctly the playing strategy. This is quite natural, since, in general, one has more time to make betting decisions. In any case, this is why we present first the betting strategy and afterward the playing strategy. The player may, of course, use the betting strategy given here and the basic strategy for playing decisions. This does not mean, however, that the player should not make the necessary effort to learn the main-count playing strategy given in the following sections. The same running index is used for both betting and playing decisions. If, in addition to the betting strategy presented in this section, the player insures when the running index is adequate and uses the main-count playing strategy his total gain will be increased (see also the remarks at the end of this section).

The bet range in the tables given below is from 1 to 12. Nevertheless, the player should be aware that in actual games he might be unable to use the tables exactly as they are written. Casino owners, pit bosses, etc., are not very happy to see skillful players and winners at their blackjack tables. Most of them know that adequate bet variation is a characteristic of skillful play. They will, probably, take action against the player who varies the amount of his bet too much and too often. This is why the player should try to "disguise" his play as much as possible (we discuss these matters further, in Chapter 5).

*When the conditions do not seem favorable the player must reduce the 1 to 12 bet range.* In single-deck games it is enough to vary the bet from 1 to 4 or from 1 to 2. In fact, the player who masters the main-count playing strategy, should be able to win in single-deck games without varying the bet. We observe, however, that when the bet range is decreased, the player's rate of gain is also decreased.

The player's expectation – that is, the player's advantage or disadvantage – depends upon the rules under which the game is played, among others. Since many rule variations are encountered in casino games, we need more than one betting table. At a given moment of play, the player's expectation also depends on the value of the running index. The betting tables given below are based on the above observations and on the relation between the increase in the running index and the corresponding change in the player's expectation. Certain practical aspects of the blackjack game were also taken into consideration in the preparation of the tables.

*Whenever we specify a set of blackjack rules, distinct from the basic rules, we generally mention only those different from the basic ones.* The basic rules were described in Chapter 2.

We shall now give the first betting table. *It should be used in four-deck games dealt from more than two decks and played under basic rules.*

**Table 1**

| BET UNITS | RUNNING INDICES |
| --- | --- |
| 1 | less than +5 |
| 2 | +5 |
| 4 | +7 |
| 8 | +10 |
| 12 | +14 |

Table 1 should be read as follows: The player should bet 1 *unit* if the running index is less than +5. He should bet 2 *units* if the running index is +5 *or more, but less than* +7. He should bet 4 *units* if the running index is +7 *or more, but less than* +10. He should bet 8 *units* if the running index is +10 *or more, but less than* +14. Finally, he should bet 12 *units* if the running index is +14 or more.

The fewer decks used in a blackjack game, the better it is for the skillful player. This is true at least in theory. Therefore, betting tables, such as the following, which take into account directly the number of unseen cards, are better.

*Most of the following tables have four columns. The second, third and fourth columns are designated by* **more than 2, 2 and 1**, *respectively.* The running indices in the second column should be used when the number of unseen cards is *greater than* 104. Those in the third column should be used when the number of unseen cards is *between* 53 *and* 104. Those in the last column should be used when the number of unseen cards is 52 *or less.*

In two-deck games the player should bet according to the running indices in the last two columns. In single-deck games he should bet according to the running indices in the last column.

**Table 2**

| BET UNITS | RUNNING INDICES | | |
|---|---|---|---|
| | more than 2 | 2 | 1 |
| 1 | less than +5 | less than +4 | less than +2 |
| 2 | +5 | +4 | +2 |
| 4 | +7 | +6 | +4 |
| 8 | +10 | +9 | +7 |
| 12 | +14 | +13 | +11 |

Table 2 replaces Table 1, when the number of unseen cards is taken into account, directly. *It should be used in games played under the basic rules.*

The explanations already given in this section show clearly how Table 2 (and other similar ones) should be read. For example, if the number of unseen cards is 150 and the running index is +6 the player should bet 2 units. If the number of unseen cards is 76 and the running index is +9, the player should bet 8 units.

In games in which, in addition to the basic rules, doubling after splitting is allowed, the player should bet according to the betting table obtained from Table 2 by decreasing the running indices by one unit. The same betting strategy should be used when, in addition to the option of doubling after splitting, surrender is also offered.

*In games in which,*

*the dealer draws to soft* 17,
*doubling down after splitting is allowed,*
*surrender is allowed,*

*the player should use betting Table 2.*

The rule which requires the dealer to draw to soft 17 is unfavorable for the player. The doubling down and surrender options are, however, favorable. When the blackjack game is played under the rules mentioned above, the player's expectation is about the same as in games played under the basic rules.

Instead of the betting scale 1, 2, 4, 8, 12, introduced in Table 2, the player may use the more conservative scale 1, 1, 2, 4, 6. He will need less capital when using the latter scale than when using the former, but his rate of gain will be substantially reduced.

#### Table 3

| BET UNITS | RUNNING INDICES | | |
|---|---|---|---|
| | more than 2 | 2 | 1 |
| 1 | less than +8 | less than +7 | less than +5 |
| 2 | +8 | +7 | +5 |
| 4 | +10 | +9 | +7 |
| 8 | +13 | +12 | +10 |
| 12 | +17 | +16 | +14 |

*In games played under the Reno–Tahoe rules, the player should bet as indicated in Table 3.*

The multiple-deck games played under the Reno–Tahoe rules are quite unfavorable for the player. Obtaining a worthwhile edge over the house in such games requires a large bet variation. The player's gain will be increased if it is possible for him to use the scale 1, 5, 10, 20, 30 instead of 1, 2, 4, 8, 12.

*In games played under British rules the player should bet according to the betting table obtained from Table 2 by increasing the indices by two units.*

*We shall also mention here the no hole-card games of type I in which:*

*doubling down on soft hands is not allowed;*
*doubling down on hard hands of value 9 or less is not allowed;*
*the dealer draws to soft 17;*
*paris can be split only once;*
*insurance is not offered.*

These are the rules under which the blackjack games are played in the Province of Alberta, Canada. They were set by the Gaming Control Section of the office of the Attorney General of the Province. These rules will be referred to as the *Province of Alberta rules.* Similar rules are encountered in other parts of the world, for example, Aruba. Games dealt under these rules should be treated as those dealt under Reno–Tahoe rules.

Among the various directives concerning blackjack issued by the Gaming Control Section of the Province of Alberta, the following deserve special attention:

The game of '21' (blackjack) shall be played with four decks of cards dealt from a dealing shoe.

After the cards are shuffled and cut a stop card shall be placed into the deck between 35 and 55 cards from the bottom, following which the cards will be placed into the shoe.

Card counters who obtain an honest advantage over the House through a playing strategy do not break any law. Gaming supervisors should ensure that no steps are taken to discourage any player simply because he is winning.

*In games played under Eastern rules the player should bet as indicated in Table 4.*

The running indices in the second column should be used when the number of unseen cards is *greater than* 104. Those in the third column, when the number of unseen cards is 104 *or less.*

The running indices in Table 4 are relatively small when compared with the corresponding ones in the other tables in this section. Therefore, in games played under Eastern rules, the player may increase the bets substantially, even when the running indices are relatively

## Table 4

| BET UNITS | RUNNING INDICES | |
|---|---|---|
| | more than 2 | 2, 1 |
| 1 | less than +1 | less than 0 |
| 2 | +1 | 0 |
| 4 | +3 | +1 |
| 8 | +6 | +5 |
| 12 | +11 | +7 |

low. The main reason for this is the early surrender option, which is very favorable to the player.

The above discussion covers the most important situations. However, because there are so many possible rule variations, we cannot give tables for all cases. In any event, on the basis of 1)-7), given below, the player should be able to determine *approximate* betting tables in most cases:

1) In games in which doubling down after splitting is allowed, the running indices should be decreased by one unit.

2) In games in which doubling on soft hands is not allowed, the running indices should be increased by one unit.

3) In games in which doubling down on hard hands of value 9 or less is not allowed, the running indices should be increased by one unit.

4) In games in which the dealer draws on soft 17, the running indices should be increased by 1.37. In practice, the running indices should be increased by one unit.

5) In games in which the player may draw to split aces, the running indices should be decreased by one unit.

6) In games in which doubling down on hard 10 is not allowed, the running indices should be increased by 3 units. This rule is *very unfavorable* to the player.

7) In no hole card games of type I the running indices should be increased by one unit.

To clarify how 1)-7) above should be used, *let us assume that we participate in a game in which:*

*doubling down on soft hands is not allowed;*

*doubling down on hard hands of value 9 or less is not allowed;*
*the dealer draws to soft 17.*

By 2), 3), *and* 4) we obtain the betting table for these rules by adding to each one of the running indices in Table 2 a total of 3 units. This leads to Table 3. This is, of course, natural, since the above are the Reno–Tahoe rules.

When *the conditions are favorable,* the player who has substantial capital should replace the betting scale

1 unit, 2 units, 4 units, 8 units, 12 units

by the scale

1 unit, 5 units, 10 units, 20 units, 30 units.

For example, if the bet unit is $5, he should use the scale

$5, $25, $50, $100, $150

Changing the bet from a $5 chip to a $25 chip might attract less attention than changing from a $5 chip to four $5 chips.

The player who decides – against our recommendations – to play in games in which special favorable rules (for example early surrender) are not offered and which are dealt from more than four decks should use the betting scale

1 unit, 5 units, 10 units, 20 units, 30 units.

At the beginning of this section we have observed that the player's total gain is increased if he uses the main-count playing strategy, which is given in the next two sections. The expectation of the basic strategy player depends on the value of the running index. The same is true when one uses the main-count playing strategy. Moreover, the expectation of this player is higher than that of the player who uses the basic strategy. If one takes this into account, some of the indices in the betting tables can be decreased. This gives the player more opportunities to bet higher and increases his overall gain. Roughly speaking, one can proceed as follows: When the running index is between 11 and 15, one should increase it by 1 before comparing it with the indices in the betting table being used. When the running index is between 16 and 20, one should increase it by 2. When the running index is between 21 and 25, one should increase it by 4. Finally, when the running index is between 26 and 30, one should increase it by 7.

## THE PLAYING STRATEGY FOR MULTIPLE-DECK GAMES

The strategy given in this section should be used for all multiple-deck games. Also, unless we say explicitly the contrary, the same strategy should be used whether the dealer stands or draws on soft 17.

The playing strategy is given in Tables 5–11. Some of the *blocks* in these tables contain *critical indices*. The player makes the playing decisions by comparing the running index with the corresponding critical index.

When a block contains two critical indices, separated by a slanted bar, the one on the left should be used *when the dealer stands on soft* 17. The one on the right should be used *when the dealer draws on soft* 17.

The player should exercise the *playing options* in the following order:

insurance;
split and resplit;
double down;
draw or stand.

When offered, the surrender option should be exercised before splitting. Early surrender should be exercised before insurance. Of course, the playing options should be exercised according to the recommendations in the following sections.

### Drawing and Standing (Hard Hands)

With a hand of value 11 or less (that is 11, 10, 9, . . .), the player should *draw,* no matter what the dealer's up card is.

With a hand of value 18 or more (that is 18, 19, . . .) the player should *stand*, no matter what the dealer's up card is.

With a hand of value 12, 13, 14, 15, 16 or 17, the player should proceed as indicated in Table 5. This table is read as follows: We determine the block, located to the *right* of the number representing the value of the player's hand and *under* the dealer's up card. If the block is *shaded*, the player should *stand*. If the block is *white, without any number on it*, the player should *draw*. If the block is *white and has a number on it,* * the player should *stand if the running index is greater than, or equal to, that number and draw otherwise.*

**Table 5**

These numbers represent the dealer's up card

These numbers represent the value of the player's hand

| | 2 | 3 | 4 | 5 | 6 | 7 | 8 | 9 | 10 | A |
|---|---|---|---|---|---|---|---|---|---|---|
| 17 | | | | | | | | | | −23/−15 |
| 16 | −32 | −35 | −40 | −45 | −50/−55 | 30 | 23 | 17 | 1 | 28/12 |
| 15 | −21 | −24 | −27 | −32 | −33/−40 | 34 | 30 | 26 | 12 | 32/18 |
| 14 | −12 | −15 | −20 | −24 | −24/−30 | 51 | | 41 | 24 | 42/28 |
| 13 | −4 | −8 | −11 | −14 | −15/−20 | | | | | |
| 12 | 9 | 5 | −1 | −6 | −3/−10 | | | | | |

For example, assume that the player's hand has the value 12 and the dealer has a 3 up. The block to the right of 12 and under 3 is white and has the number 5 on it. Hence, the player should stand if the running index is 5 or more (that is, 5, 6, 7, . . .) and draw otherwise.

### Drawing and Standing (Soft Hands)

The player should follow the basic strategy, *except in the case when the dealer has an ace up.* Hence, when the dealer's up card is

$$2, 3, 4, 5, 6, 7, \text{ or } 8$$

---

*This is the *critical index* for the corresponding situation.

*the player should draw to any soft hand of value* 17 *or less and stand otherwise.* When the dealer's up card is

9 or ten

*the player should draw to any soft hand of value* 18 *or less and stand otherwise.*

Now assume that *the dealer has an ace up.* The player should *always* stand on 19 or more and draw on 17 or less. When the dealer *stands on soft* 17, the player should *stand on soft* 18, *if the running index is greater than, or equal to,*

3

*and draw otherwise.* When the dealer *draws on soft* 17, *the player should again follow the basic strategy.* Therefore he should *draw on soft* 18.

### Doubling Down (Hard Hands)

The player should consider doubling only when his hand has the value 7, 8, 9, 10, or 11. When the player should double is indicated in Table 6. This table is read as follows: We determine the block to the *right* of the number representing the value of the player's hand and *under* the dealer's up card. If the block is *shaded* the player *should not double.* If the block is *white, without any number on it,* the player *should double down.* If the block *is white, with a number*

Table 6

These numbers represent the dealer's up card

| value of player's hand | 2 | 3 | 4 | 5 | 6 | 7 | 8 | 9 | 10 | A |
|---|---|---|---|---|---|---|---|---|---|---|
| 11 | −45 | −50 | −52 | −60 | −65 | −36 | −26 | −17 | −17 | 3/−2 |
| 10 | −35 | −38 | −41 | −50 | −55 | −25 | −17 | −6 | 12 | 12/10 |
| 9 | 3 | −3 | −11 | −16 | −22 | 11 | 26 | | | |
| 8 | 44 | 30 | 20 | 12 | 8 | 50 | | | | |
| 7 | | | 45 | 38 | 38 | | | | | |

These numbers represent the value of the player's hand

*on it, the player should double only when the running index is greater than or equal to that number.*

For example, assume that the player's hand has the value 10 and the dealer has a 9 up. The block to the right of 10 and under 9 is white and has the number –6 on it. Hence, the player should double in this case only if the running index is –6 or more.

### Doubling Down (Soft Hands)

The player should consider doubling only when his hand has the value 13, 14, 15, 16, 17, 18, 19, or 20. Since, in general, one can double only on the initial two-card hand, this means that the player should consider doubling only when he has (A, 2), (A, 3), (A, 4), (A, 5), (A, 6), (A, 7), (A, 8) and (A, 9). When the player should double with such a hand, is indicated in Table 7.

**Table 7**

These numbers represent the dealer's up card

| | 2 | 3 | 4 | 5 | 6 | 7 | 8 | 9 | 10 | A |
|----|----|----|----|----|----|----|----|----|----|----|
| **20** | 31 | 27 | 21 | 17 | 17 | | | | | |
| **19** | 23 | 17 | 10 | 5 | 3/–2 | | | | | |
| **18** | 2 | –6 | –15 | –21 | –24/–34 | | | | | |
| **17** | 2 | –9 | –20 | –30 | –47 | | | | | |
| **16** | | 7 | –7 | –22 | –47 | | | | | |
| **15** | | 14 | –2 | –17 | –40 | | | | | |
| **14** | 40 | 17 | 4 | –9 | –23 | | | | | |
| **13** | 27 | 17 | 9 | –1 | –11 | | | | | |

These numbers represent the value of the player's hand

Observe that the block to the *right* of 19 and *under* 6 contains two critical indices, 3 and –2. When the dealer *stands on soft* 17, the player *should double on* (A 8) *against a* 6, *only if the running index is greater than, or equal to,* 3. When the dealer *draws on soft* 17, the player *should double on* (A, 8) *against a* 6, *only if the running index is –2 or more.*

Otherwise, read Table 7, in the same manner as Table 6.

Dealers, and other players, will often criticize your play if you double on (A, 9) against 6, for example: You will be told: "You already had 20! What else do you want?" Do not listen to these *smart persons* and do not try to explain why you doubled down. Calculations have shown that it is to your advantage to follow the strategy recommended in Table 6.

### Splitting (When Doubling After Splitting Is Not Allowed)

The strategy for splitting pairs is given in Table 8. This table is read as follows: We determine the block located to the *right* of the numbers representing the player's pair and *under* the dealer's up card. If the block is *shaded*, the player *should not split*. If the block is *white, without any number on it*, the player *should split*. If the block is *white and has a number on it, the player should split only when the running index is greater than or equal to that number*.

There is, however, an *exception* to this rule. If the number in the block is followed by a dot, *the player should split only when the running index is less than that number*.

### Table 8

These numbers represent the dealer's up card

| | 2 | 3 | 4 | 5 | 6 | 7 | 8 | 9 | 10 | A |
|------|-----|-----|-----|-----|---------|------|------|------|------|------|
| A, A | −45 | −45 | | | | −35 | −29 | −29 | −27 | −19 |
| 10, 10 | 37 | 28 | 21 | 17 | 17 | 50 | | | | |
| 9, 9 | −4 | −8 | −12 | −15 | −15/−19 | 30 | | | | 12/8 |
| 8, 8 | | | | | | | | | 20• | |
| 7, 7 | −35 | −35 | −60 | | | | | | | |
| 6, 6 | 5 | −5 | −11 | −19 | −27 | | | | | |
| 5, 5 | | | | | | | | | | |
| 4, 4 | | − | | | | | | | | |
| 3, 3 | 44 | 9 | −2 | −12 | | | 35• | | | |
| 2, 2 | 29 | 8 | −1 | −11 | | | | | | |

These numbers represent the player's pair

For example, the player should split (9, 9) against a dealer's 7 if the running index is 30 or more. He should split (8, 8) against a 10 only if the running index is less than 20. When surrender is offered the player should surrender (8, 8) against a 10 when the running index is 6 or more.

### Splitting (When Doubling Down After Splitting Is Allowed)

The corresponding strategy is given in Table 9. This table is read in the same way as Table 8.

**Table 9**

These numbers represent the dealer's up card

| | 2 | 3 | 4 | 5 | 6 | 7 | 8 | 9 | 10 | A |
|---|---|---|---|---|---|---|---|---|---|---|
| A, A | | | | AS IN TABLE 8 | | | | | | |
| 10, 10 | | | | AS IN TABLE 8 | | | | | | |
| 9, 9 | −8 | −13 | −18 | −23 | −24/−30 | 20 | | | | 12/7 |
| 8, 8 | | | | | | | | | 30● | |
| 7, 7 | | | | | | 4 | | | | |
| 6, 6 | −9 | −15 | −21 | −27 | | | | | | |
| 5, 5 | | | | | | | | | | |
| 4, 4 | | 28 | 12 | −2 | −6 | | | | | |
| 3, 3 | −5 | −23 | | | | | | | | |
| 2, 2 | −12 | −19 | −24 | −30 | | | 20 | | | |

These numbers represent the player's pair

For example, the player should split (9, 9) against a dealer's 7 if the running index is 20 or more. He should split (8, 8) against a 10 if the running index is less than 30.

Observe that, in general, the critical indices in Table 9 are smaller than the corresponding ones in Table 8. Hence, the player will split more often when doubling after splitting is allowed.

## Insurance

The player should place the insurance bet only *when the running index is greater than or equal to*

$$9$$

We have assumed above that the game is dealt from a four-deck shoe. When the number of decks used in the game is different, 9 should be replaced by the following indices:

|                   |    |
|-------------------|----|
| six-deck games    | 10 |
| two-deck games    | 8  |
| one-deck games    | 6  |

For example, in single-deck games the player should insure only if the running index is greater than or equal to 6.

## Surrender

When the option may be exercised *only after it was determined that the dealer does not have blackjack,* the player should follow the strategy given in Table 10. When *early surrender* is offered, the player should follow the strategy given in Table 11.

### Table 10

These numbers represent the dealer's up card

These numbers represent the player's hand

|      | 8  | 9  | 10 | A  |
|------|----|----|----|----|
| 17   |    | 38 | 38 |    |
| 16   | 20 | 0  | −9 | −4 |
| 8, 8 |    | 30 | 6  |    |
| 15   | 24 | 8  | −2 | 4  |
| 14   | 35 | 19 | 12 | 19 |
| 7, 7 | 32 | 15 | 9  | 13 |
| 13   |    | 35 | 25 | 37 |

**Table 11**

These numbers represent
the dealer's up card

| | 8 | 9 | 10 | A |
|---|---|---|---|---|
| 17 | | 38 | 21 | |
| 16 | 20 | 0 | −21 | |
| 8, 8 | | 30 | −8 | |
| 15 | 24 | 8 | −12 | |
| 14 | 35 | 19 | −2 | |
| 7, 7 | 32 | 15 | −7 | |
| 13 | | 35 | 10 | −42 |
| 12 | | | 25 | −28 |
| 7 | | | 50 | −28 |
| 6 | | | 40 | −11 |
| 5 | | | 50 | 0 |
| 4 | | | 50 | 0 |

These numbers
represent the
player's hand

Tables 10 and 11 are read as follows: We determine the block located to the *right* of the number (or numbers) representing the player's hand and *under* the dealer's up card. If the block is *shaded*, the player *should not surrender*. If the block is *white, without any number on it*, the player *should surrender*. If the block is *white, with a number on it*, the player *should surrender only when the running index is greater than that number*.

Assume, for example, that the player follows the strategy given in Table 11, that he has hard 17 and that the dealer's up card is an ace. In this case he should surrender. If the dealer's up card is a 10, he should surrender only if the running index is 21 or more.

### No Hole Card Games

In *no hole-card games of type I* the player should proceed as follows: When the dealer's up card is

2, 3, 4, 5, 6, 7, 8, or 9

the playing strategy remains unchanged. When the dealer's up card is

ten or ace

the following modifications should be made to the strategy given previously:

do not split (8, 8) against a ten or ace;

do not split (9, 9) against an ace;

do not split (A, A) against an ace;

split (A, A) against a ten, only if the running index is greater than or equal to –20;

do not double on ten against a ten or ace;

double on 11 against a ten only if the running index is greater than or equal to 40;

do not double on 11 against an ace.

In *no hole-card games of type II* the player should follow the strategy given earlier in this chapter.

## THE PLAYING STRATEGY FOR SINGLE-DECK GAMES

As in the case of the basic strategy, there are a number of differences in the playing strategies, for multiple-deck and single-deck games, corresponding to a point-count system. Strictly speaking, many of the critical indices change when the number of unseen cards change. Nevertheless, we do not intend to give new sets of critical indices and to recommend that the reader learn them. For various reasons, this would not be justified. The player should use, in general, the indices in the tables given for multiple-deck games. Some of these indices have been rounded so that they correspond better to various situations one encounters in actual games. In any case a few of the critical indices for multiple-deck games are listed in the third column of Table 12. They should replace the corresponding ones in the tables for multiple-deck games. For example, assume that the player has hard 12 and the dealer's up card is a 2. The corresponding critical index for multiple-deck games is 9. The index for single-deck games is 12.

## Table 12

| PLAYER'S HAND | DEALER'S UP CARD | CRITICAL INDICES |
|---|---|---|
| *Drawing and standing* | | |
| hard 12 | 2 | 12 |
| soft 18 | A | -7/27 |
| *Doubling down (Hard hands)* | | |
| 11 | A | -2/-4 |
| 9 | 2 | 2 |
| 8 | 6 | 10 |
| *Doubling down (Soft hands)* | | |
| (A, 7) | 2 | 4 |
| (A, 6) | 2 | 0 |
| (A, 3) | 4 | -5 |
| (A, 2) | 4 | 2 |
| *Splitting (when doubling down after splitting is allowed)* | | |
| (3, 3) or (7, 7) | 8 | split |
| (6, 6) | 7 | split |
| *Surrender* | | |
| 16 | 9 | 5 |
| (7, 7) | 10 | -6 |

## ADJUSTED COUNTS

By *correcting* for 5s and aces and by introducing an adjusted running index, we can improve slightly the *betting performance*, already excellent, of the main-count system. We correct for 5s and aces by using the count* defined by:

| 2 | 3 | 4 | 5 | 6 | 7 | 8 | 9 | 10 | A |
|---|---|---|---|---|---|---|---|---|---|
| 0 | 0 | 0 | +1 | 0 | 0 | 0 | 0 | 0 | -1 |

$$(3)$$

To simplify the discussion below, we denote by MC and FA the running counts corresponding, respectively, to the main count and to the count defined by (3).

---

*In Ref. 47, K. Uston gave a blackjack system based on this count. Its performance is evaluated in Ref. 23, p. 45.

In actual games the player should calculate MC and FA separately. The *adjusted running index* is

$$\frac{(MC + FA) \times 100}{\text{number of unseen cards}} \qquad (4)$$

An approximate value of this index can be obtained by one of the methods described in Chapter 5.

*Example.* – Assume that the game is dealt from a two-deck pack and that the cards we have seen are:

one 3, three 5s, three 6s, one 8, four tens, and, one ace.

Then

$$MC = 4 \text{ and } FA = 2$$

The number of unseen cards is

$$91(= 104 - 13).$$

The *running index* corresponding to MC is

$$\frac{4 \times 100}{91} = \text{about 4.}$$

*The adjusted running index* is

$$\frac{(4 + 2) \times 100}{91} = \text{about 6}$$

and gives a better estimation of the player's advantage.

The player who keeps track of the adjusted running index should make the betting decisions by using this index and the betting tables given earlier in this chapter.

We observe that the index (4) is the running index corresponding to the count defined by the table

| 2 | 3 | 4 | 5 | 6 | 7 | 8 | 9 | 10 | A |
|----|----|----|----|----|----|----|----|----|----|
| +1 | +1 | +2 | +3 | +2 | +1 | 0 | 0 | -2 | -2 |

By *correcting* for 9s and aces and by using a corresponding adjusted running index, we can improve the *playing performance* of the main-count system. We shall not give further details. We shall only observe that the adjusted running index mentioned here is the running index corresponding to the count defined by:

| 2 | 3 | 4 | 5 | 6 | 7 | 8 | 9 | 10 | A |
|---|---|---|---|---|---|---|---|----|---|
| +1 | +1 | +2 | +2 | +2 | +1 | 0 | −1 | −2 | 0 |

This count was introduced by P. Griffin (see Ref. 13, p. 244).

THE MAIN-COUNT SYSTEM
THE APPROXIMATE PLAYING STRATEGY FOR MULTIPLE-DECK GAMES

DRAW STAND (HARD HAND)

|    | 2 | 3 | 4 | 5 | 6 | 7 | 8 | 9 | 10 | A |
|----|---|---|---|---|---|---|---|---|----|---|
| 17 |   |   |   |   |   |   |   |   |    |   |
| 16 |   |   |   |   |   |   |   | 17 | 1 |   |
| 15 |   |   |   |   |   |   |   |   | 12 |   |
| 14 | −12 | −15 | −20 |   |   |   |   |   | 24 |   |
| 13 | −4 | −8 | −11 | −14 | −15/−20 |   |   |   |    |   |
| 12 | 9 | 5 | −1 | −6 | −3/−10 |   |   |   |    |   |

DRAW STAND (SOFT HANDS)
When the dealer's up card is 2, 3, 4, 5, 6, 7 or 8, the player should draw to any soft hand of value 17 or less and stand otherwise. When the dealer's up card is 9 or Ten, the player should draw to any soft hand of value 18 or less and stand otherwise. Assume now the dealer has an Ace up: The player should always draw on 17 or less and stand on 19 or more. When the dealer <u>stands on soft 17</u>, the player should stand on soft 18 if the running index is 3 or more and draw otherwise. When the dealer <u>draws on soft</u> 17, the player should draw on soft 18.

DOUBLING DOWN (HARD HANDS)

|    | 2 | 3 | 4 | 5 | 6 | 7 | 8 | 9 | 10 | A |
|----|---|---|---|---|---|---|---|---|----|---|
| 11 |   |   |   |   |   |   |   | −17 | −17 | 3/−2 |
| 10 |   |   |   |   |   |   | −17 | −6 | 12 | 12/10 |
| 9  | 3 | −3 | −11 | −16 |   | 11 |   |   |    |   |
| 8  |   |   | 20 | 12 | 8 |   |   |   |    |   |
| 7  |   |   |   |   |   |   |   |   |    |   |

DOUBLING DOWN (SOFT HANDS)

|    | 2 | 3  | 4   | 5   | 6      | 7 | 8 | 9 | 10 | A |
|----|---|----|-----|-----|--------|---|---|---|----|---|
| 20 |   |    |     | 17  | 17     |   |   |   |    |   |
| 19 |   | 17 | 10  | 5   | 3/−2   |   |   |   |    |   |
| 18 | 2 | −6 | −15 |     |        |   |   |   |    |   |
| 17 | 2 | −9 |     |     |        |   |   |   |    |   |
| 16 |   | 7  | −7  |     |        |   |   |   |    |   |
| 15 |   | 14 | −2  | −17 |        |   |   |   |    |   |
| 14 |   | 17 | 4   | −9  |        |   |   |   |    |   |
| 13 |   | 17 | 9   | −1  | −11    |   |   |   |    |   |

SPLITTING (WHEN DOUBLING DOWN AFTER SPLITTING IS NOT ALLOWED)

|        | 2  | 3  | 4   | 5   | 6        | 7 | 8 | 9 | 10   | A     |
|--------|----|----|-----|-----|----------|---|---|---|------|-------|
| A, A   |    |    |     |     |          |   |   |   |      | −19   |
| 10, 10 |    |    | 21  | 17  | 17       |   |   |   |      |       |
| 9, 9   | −4 | −8 | −12 | −15 | −15/−19  |   |   |   |      | 12/8  |
| 8, 8   |    |    |     |     |          |   |   |   | 20●  |       |
| 7, 7   |    |    |     |     |          |   |   |   |      |       |
| 6, 6   | 5  | −5 | −11 | −19 |          |   |   |   |      |       |
| 5, 5   |    |    |     |     |          |   |   |   |      |       |
| 4, 4   |    |    |     |     |          |   |   |   |      |       |
| 3, 3   |    | 9  | −2  | −12 |          |   |   |   |      |       |
| 2, 2   |    | 8  | −1  | −11 |          |   |   |   |      |       |

SPLITTING (WHEN DOUBLING DOWN AFTER SPLITTING IS ALLOWED)

|        | 2   | 3   | 4   | 5   | 6   | 7  | 8  | 9 | 10 | A     |
|--------|-----|-----|-----|-----|-----|----|----|---|----|-------|
| A, A   | AS IN THE ABOVE TABLE |     |     |     |     |    |    |   |    |       |
| 10, 10 | AS IN THE ABOVE TABLE |     |     |     |     |    |    |   |    |       |
| 9, 9   | −8  | −13 | −18 |     |     | 20 |    |   |    | 12/7  |
| 8, 8   |     |     |     |     |     |    |    |   |    |       |
| 7, 7   |     |     |     |     |     |    | 4  |   |    |       |
| 6, 6   | −9  | −15 | −21 |     |     |    |    |   |    |       |
| 5, 5   |     |     |     |     |     |    |    |   |    |       |
| 4, 4   |     |     | 12  | −2  | −6  |    |    |   |    |       |
| 3, 3   | −5  |     |     |     |     |    |    |   |    |       |
| 2, 2   | −12 | −19 |     |     |     |    | 20 |   |    |       |

SURRENDER

|       | 8  | 9  | 10 | A  |
|-------|----|----|----|----|
| 17    |    |    |    |    |
| 16    | 20 | 0  | −9 | −4 |
| 8, 8  |    | 30 | 6  |    |
| 15    | 24 | 8  | −2 | 4  |
| 14    |    | 19 | 12 | 19 |
| 7, 7  |    | 15 | 9  | 13 |
| 13    |    |    | 25 |    |

EARLY SURRENDER

|       | 8  | 9  | 10  | A   |
|-------|----|----|-----|-----|
| 17    |    | 1  | 21  |     |
| 16    | 20 | 0  | −21 |     |
| 8, 8  |    |    |     | −8  |
| 15    |    | 8  | −12 |     |
| 14    |    | 19 | −2  |     |
| 7, 7  |    | 15 | −7  |     |
| 13    |    |    | 10  |     |
| 12    |    |    |     |     |
| 7     |    |    |     |     |
| 6     |    |    |     | −11 |
| 5     |    |    |     | 0   |
| 4     |    |    |     | 0   |

INSURANCE
The player should insure only when the running index is 9 or more

# 4
# The 99-Count System and the Adjusted Count System

In this chapter we describe the *99-count system*. As in the case of the main-count system we give corresponding betting and playing strategies.

The 99-count is better than the main-count for making betting decisions. The main-count, however, is better for making playing decisions. The player who does not *correct* the count he uses might prefer the main-count. This assumes, however, that he will vary the playing strategy according to the count. The player who varies the playing strategy only occasionally and otherwise uses the basic strategy will be better off using the 99-count, particularly in multiple-deck games.

By *correcting* the 99-count for tens and aces we obtain the *adjusted count*. We discuss this count in the section, *The 99-count and the Adjusted count*. The corresponding playing strategy can be found at the end of this chapter. We did not give betting strategies for the adjusted count since we do not recommend that this count be used without *corrections*. The adjusted count should be used mainly, for playing decisions. The player who can use the 99-count for betting decisions and the adjusted count for playing decisions will obtain better results than those obtained by the use of most other blackjack systems. Nevertheless, this player will not have a major advantage over the one who perfectly plays the main-count system.

## THE 99-COUNT SYSTEM

The 99-*count* is defined by the following:

| 2 | 3 | 4 | 5 | 6 | 7 | 8 | 9 | 10 | A |
|---|---|---|---|---|---|---|---|----|---|
| +2 | +2 | +2 | +3 | +2 | +1 | 0 | -1 | -2 | -3 |

On the first line, we listed the cards and under each card the value associated with it. As in the case of the main-count, the numbers associated with the cards are called *weights*.* For example, the weight of an ace is –1, in the main-count. The weight of an ace is –3, in the 99-count.

Whatever the count is, the corresponding *running count* and *running index* are introduced as in the case of the main-count (see Chapter 3).

*Example.* – Assume that the game is dealt from a four-deck shoe and that the first six cards we have seen are

$$7, 3, 7, 5, 5, \text{king}$$

The corresponding *running count* is

$$+1+2+1+3+3+(-2) = +8$$

The number of unseen cards is

$$202 \ (=208–6)$$

whence, the *running index* is

$$\frac{+8 \times 100}{202} = \text{about} +4$$

---

*This terminology is used, in this book, no matter what the count is.

If, for instance, 50 cards were dealt and seen, the number of unseen cards is

$$158 \, (=208-50);$$

if the corresponding *running count* is +23, the *running index* is

$$\frac{+23 \times 100}{158} = \text{about } +14.$$

*Methods of computing the running index during actual play are discussed in Chapter 5.*

As in the case of the main-count, we observe that, in *general*:*

When the *running count* is a large positive number, there is an excess of high cards among the unseen cards.

When the *running count* is a small negative number, there is an excess of low cards among the unseen cards.

As we already wrote in the previous chapter, the strategies corresponding to point count systems, particularly the strategy corresponding to the 99-count system, are based, in fact, on the above remarks.

The player should exercise the playing options in the same order as in the case of the main-count system.

## THE BETTING STRATEGY

We discuss in this section the betting strategy corresponding to the *99-count*.

Most of the general remarks made in Chapter 3, in the section, *The betting strategy,* are valid here. They will not be repeated. The betting tables given in this section are set the same way as the corresponding tables in Chapter 3. They should be read in the same manner. The betting table for *games played under the basic rules is Table 1*.

*The betting table for games in which the player may double after splitting is obtained from Table 1 by decreasing the running indices by one unit.* The same table should be used when, in addition to the option of doubling down, surrender is also offered.

---

*These remarks remain valid, no matter what the count system is.

**Table 1**

| BET UNITS | RUNNING INDICES | | |
|---|---|---|---|
| | more than 2 | 2 | 1 |
| 1 | less than +6 | less than +5 | less than +2 |
| 2 | +6 | +5 | +2 |
| 4 | +8 | +7 | +4 |
| 8 | +12 | +11 | +8 |
| 12 | +16 | +15 | +12 |

*In games in which,*

*the dealer draws on soft 17,*
*doubling down after splitting is allowed,*
*surrender is allowed,*

*the player should use Table 1.*

This would be an excellent set of rules if the dealer would not be required to draw to soft 17.

*In games played under the Reno–Tahoe rules the player should use Table 2.*

**Table 2**

| BET UNITS | RUNNING INDICES | | |
|---|---|---|---|
| | more than | 2 | 1 |
| 1 | less than +9 | less than +8 | less than +6 |
| 2 | +9 | +8 | +6 |
| 4 | +12 | +11 | +8 |
| 8 | +15 | +14 | +12 |
| 12 | +19 | +18 | +16 |

Observe that the betting strategy for single-deck games played under Reno–Tahoe rules is identical to that for four-deck games played under basic rules.

*In games played under British rules, the player should bet according to the betting table obtained from Table 1 by increasing the indices by two units.*

*In games played under Eastern rules the player should use Table 3.*

### Table 3

| BET UNITS | | RUNNING INDICES |
|---|---|---|
| more than 2 | | **2, 1** |
| 1 | less than +1 | less than 0 |
| 2 | +1 | 0 |
| 4 | +3 | +1 |
| 8 | +7 | +5 |
| 12 | +12 | +10 |

To obtain betting tables for games played under rules not discussed here, the player should use 1)–7) in the section, *The betting strategy*, in Chapter 3.

The player who used the 90-count playing strategy can adjust the running index, for betting purposes, in the following manner (see the end of the section on betting in the previous chapter): When the running index is between 11 and 15 he should increase it by 1 before comparing it with the indices in the betting table he is using. When it is between 16 and 20 he should increase it by 2. When it is between 21 and 25 he should increase by 3. Finally, when it is between 26 and 30 he should increase it by 6.

### THE PLAYING STRATEGY FOR
### MULTIPLE-DECK GAMES

The strategy given in this section should be used for all multiple-deck games. Also, unless stated explicitly the contrary, the same strategy should be used whether the dealer stands or draws on soft 17.

The playing strategy is given in Tables 4–10. These tables should be read as those in Chapter 3. Therefore, when a block in one of Tables 4–10, contains a *critical index*, the player should make the corresponding playing decision by comparing the running index with the critical index in the block. When a block contains two critical indices, the one on the left should be used *when the dealer stands on soft* 17. The one on the right should be used *when the dealer draws on soft* 17.

### Drawing and Standing (Hard Hands)

With a hand of value 11 or less (that is 11, 10, 9, . . .), the player should *draw*, no matter what the dealer's up card is.

With a hand of value 18 or more (that is 18, 19, . . .), the player should *stand*, no matter what the dealer's up card is.

With a hand of value 12, 13, 14, 15, 16, or 17, the player should proceed as indicated in Table 4.*

#### Table 4

These numbers represent
the dealer's up card

| | 2 | 3 | 4 | 5 | 6 | 7 | 8 | 9 | 10 | A |
|---|---|---|---|---|---|---|---|---|---|---|
| 17 | | | | | | | | | | −33/−22 |
| 16 | −44 | −47 | −52 | −55 | −70/−75 | 33 | 28 | 21 | 1 | 35/14 |
| 15 | −29 | −33 | −37 | −42 | −49/−57 | 43 | 41 | 36 | 17 | 44/24 |
| 14 | −17 | −22 | −27 | −32 | −36/−43 | 70 | | 60 | 37 | 60/40 |
| 13 | −5 | −10 | −16 | −21 | −24/−30 | | | | | |
| 12 | 15 | 7 | −1 | −8 | −6/−18 | | | | | |

These numbers represent the player's hand

For example, assume that the player's hand has the value 12 and the dealer's up card is a 6. When the dealer stands on soft 17, the player should stand if the running index is −6 or more (that is −6, −5, −4, . . .) and draw otherwise. When the dealer draws on soft 17, the player should stand if the running index is −18 or more (that is −18, −17, −16, . . .) and draw otherwise.

---

*As we already wrote, Table 4 and the other tables in this chapter should be read in the same way as the corresponding ones in Chapter 3.

### Drawing and Standing (Soft Hands)

The player should follow the basic strategy, *except when the dealer has an ace up.* When the dealer's up card is an ace, the player should proceed as follows: He should *always* stand on 19 or more and draw on soft 17 or less. When the dealer *stands* on soft 17, the player should *stand on soft* 18 *if the running count is*

$$+6$$

*or more, and draw otherwise.* When the dealer *draws* on soft 17, the player should *draw on soft* 18.

### Doubling Down (Hard Hands)

The player should consider doubling only when his hand has the value 7, 8, 9, 10, or 11. When the player should double is indicated in Table 5.

#### Table 5

These numbers represent the dealer's up card

| | 2 | 3 | 4 | 5 | 6 | 7 | 8 | 9 | 10 | A |
|---|---|---|---|---|---|---|---|---|---|---|
| 11 | | | | | | −50 | −35 | −27 | −27 | 4/−4 |
| 10 | −50 | −53 | −57 | −65 | −70 | −30 | −21 | −9 | 16 | 16/12 |
| 9 | 4 | −4 | −13 | −20 | −30 | 13 | 32 | | | |
| 8 | 60 | 39 | 24 | 16 | 9 | 65 | | | | |
| 7 | | | 60 | 50 | 55 | | | | | |

These numbers represent the player's hand

For example, assume that the player's hand has the value 10 and the dealer has a ten up. If the dealer does not have blackjack, the player should double only if the running index is +16 or more (that is +16, +17, +18, . . .).

**Doubling Down (Soft Hands)**

The player should consider doubling only when his hand has the value 13, 14, 15, 16, 17, 18, 19, or 20. Since, in general, one can double only on the initial two-card hands, this means that the player should consider doubling only when he has (A, 2), (A, 3), (A, 4), (A, 5), (A, 6), (A, 7), (A, 8), or (A, 9). When the player should double with such a hand is indicated in Table 6.

**Table 6**

These numbers represent the dealer's up card

These numbers represent the value of the player's hand

| | 2 | 3 | 4 | 5 | 6 | 7 | 8 | 9 | 10 | A |
|---|---|---|---|---|---|---|---|---|---|---|
| 20 | 40 | 35 | 27 | 20 | 18 | | | | | |
| 19 | 34 | 20 | 11 | 7 | 2/−3 | | | | | |
| 18 | 2 | −10 | −25 | −35 | −47/−59 | | | | | |
| 17 | 2 | −16 | −32 | −50 | | | | | | |
| 16 | | 12 | −15 | −35 | | | | | | |
| 15 | | 25 | −4 | −26 | | | | | | |
| 14 | | 28 | 5 | −14 | −34 | | | | | |
| 13 | 50 | 28 | 12 | −2 | −12/−16 | | | | | |

**Splitting (When Doubling After
Splitting Is Not Allowed)**

The strategy for splitting pairs is given in Table 7. When the number in a block is followed by a dot, the player *should split only when the running index is less than that number.*

**Splitting (When Doubling After
Splitting Is Allowed)**

The corresponding strategy is given in Table 8.

## Table 7

These numbers represent
the dealer's up card

| | | 2 | 3 | 4 | 5 | 6 | 7 | 8 | 9 | 10 | A |
|---|---|---|---|---|---|---|---|---|---|---|---|
| | A, A | −57 | −57 | | | | −55 | −48 | −48 | −45 | −28 |
| | T, T | 45 | 35 | 25 | 21 | 21 | 60 | | | | |
| | 9, 9 | −5 | −11 | −16 | −20 | −20/−27 | 30 | | | | 13/8 |
| | 8, 8 | | | | | | | | | 30• | |
| These numbers represent the player's hand | 7, 7 | −55 | −55 | | | | | | | | |
| | 6, 6 | 6 | −6 | −20 | −25 | −35 | | | | | |
| | 5, 5 | | | | | | | | | | |
| | 4, 4 | | | | | | | | | | |
| | 3, 3 | | 14 | −3 | −15 | | 45• | | | | |
| | 2, 2 | 37 | 10 | −1 | −12 | | | | | | |

## Table 8

These numbers represent
the dealer's up card

| | | 2 | 3 | 4 | 5 | 6 | 7 | 8 | 9 | 10 | A |
|---|---|---|---|---|---|---|---|---|---|---|---|
| | A, A | | | | AS IN TABLE 7 | | | | | | |
| | T, T | | | | AS IN TABLE 7 | | | | | | |
| | 9, 9 | −11 | −20 | −25 | −30 | −32/−42 | 15 | | | | 13/7 |
| | 8, 8 | | | | | | | | | 37• | |
| These numbers represent the player's hand | 7, 7 | −55 | −55 | | | | | 9 | | | |
| | 6, 6 | −11 | −18 | −29 | −37 | −42 | | | | | |
| | 5, 5 | | | | | | | | | | |
| | 4, 4 | | 34 | 12 | −5 | −15 | | | | | |
| | 3, 3 | −7 | −27 | −40 | −46 | | | | | | |
| | 2, 2 | −17 | −25 | −33 | −43 | | | 23 | | | |

### Insurance

The player should place the insurance bet only *when the running index is greater than, or equal to*

$$+14$$

We have assumed above that the game is dealt from a four-deck shoe. When the number of decks used in the game is different, 14 should be replaced by the following indices:

six-deck games   15
two-deck games   12
one-deck games   7

### Surrender

When the option may be exercised *only after it was determined that the dealer does not have blackjack,* the player should follow the strategy given in Table 9. When *early surrender* is offered, the player should follow the strategy given in Table 10.

**Table 9**

These numbers represent the dealer's up card

These numbers represent the player's hand

|       | 8  | 9   | 10  | A   |
|-------|----|-----|-----|-----|
| 17    |    | 47  | 47  |     |
| 16    | 20 | −1  | −13 | −7  |
| 8, 8  |    | 37  | 7   |     |
| 15    | 30 | 10  | −1  | 5   |
| 14    | 40 | 23  | 14  | 23  |
| 7, 7  | 37 | 20  | 9   | 18  |
| 13    |    | 45  | 30  | 45  |

**Table 10**

These numbers represent the dealer's up card

These numbers represent the player's hand

|       | 8  | 9   | 10  | A   |
|-------|----|-----|-----|-----|
| 17    |    | 47  | 25  |     |
| 16    | 20 | −1  | −25 |     |
| 8, 8  |    | 37  | −8  |     |
| 15    | 30 | 10  | −12 |     |
| 14    | 40 | 23  | −2  |     |
| 7, 7  | 37 | 20  | −4  |     |
| 13    |    | 45  | 12  | −60 |
| 12    |    |     | 30  | −40 |
| 7     |    |     | 60  | −40 |
| 6     |    |     | 50  | −20 |
| 5     |    |     | 60  | 0   |
| 4     |    |     | 60  | 0   |

The early surrender option should be exercised before the insurance option.

### No Hole-Card Games

*In no hole-card games of type I,* the modifications in the player's strategy are identical with those indicated in Chapter 3, except in the case of (A, A) and hard 11 against a dealer's ten. In any case to facilitate the reading of this subsection, we provide complete details.

When the dealer's up card is

$$2, 3, 4, 5, 6, 7, 8, \text{or } 9$$

the playing strategy remains unchanged. When the dealer's up card is

$$\text{ten or ace}$$

the following modifications should be made to the strategy given previously:

    do not split (8, 8) against a ten or ace;

    do not split (9, 9) against an ace;

    do not split (A, A) against an ace;

    split (A, A) against a ten, only if the running index is greater than or equal to –25;

    do not double on ten against a ten or ace;

    double on 11 against a ten only if the running index is greater than or equal to +48;

    do not double on 11 against an ace

*In no hole-card games of type II* the player should use the strategy given earlier in this chapter.

### THE PLAYING STRATEGY FOR
### SINGLE-DECK GAMES

Although the strategies for multiple-deck and single-deck games are similar, there are, however, a number of differences. Some of them are listed in Table 11 below.

### Table 11

| PLAYER'S HAND | DEALER'S UP CARD | CRITICAL INDICES |
|---|---|---|
| *Drawing and standing* | | |
| hard 12 | 3 | 6 |
| soft 18 | A | –12/42 |
| *Doubling down (Hard hands)* | | |
| 11 | A | –7/–14 |
| 8 | 6 | 12 |
| *Doubling down (Soft hands)* | | |
| (A, 8) | 6 | –3 |
| (A, 6) | 2 | –4 |
| (A, 3) | 4 | –11 |
| (A, 2) | 4 | 0 |
| *Splitting (when doubling after splitting is not allowed)* | | |
| (A, A) | A | –45 |
| *Splitting (when doubling after splitting is allowed)* | | |
| (3, 3) or (7, 7) | 8 | split |
| (6, 6) | 7 | split |
| *Surrender* | | |
| 16 | 9 | 7 |
| (7, 7) | 10 | –6 |

The numbers in the third column are *critical indices*. They replace those corresponding to multiple-deck games.

### THE 99-COUNT AND THE ADJUSTED-COUNT

We discuss below the count defined by:

$$\begin{array}{c|c|c|c|c|c|c|c|c|c|c}
2 & 3 & 4 & 5 & 6 & 7 & 8 & 9 & 10 & A \\
\hline
+2 & +2 & +2 & +3 & +2 & +1 & 0 & -1 & -3 & 1
\end{array} \tag{5}$$

To facilitate reference we shall call it the *adjusted-count*. The name is justified since this count can be obtained by *correcting* the 99-count for tens and aces.

The adjusted-count is excellent for making playing decisions. The corresponding strategy tables can be found at the end of this chapter.

The player who can use the 99-count for betting decisions and the adjusted-count for playing decisions will improve his overall strategy. We observe, however, that the betting performance of the adjusted-count is not as good as that of the 99-count. The adjusted-count should not be used without *corrections,* unless, for various reasons, the player must bet always the same amount.

The player who decides to use the 99-count *and* the adjusted-count, should proceed as follows: He should start by keeping track of the running count corresponding to the adjusted-count; denote this running count by AC. Then, he should keep track, separately, of the running count corresponding to the count defined by:

| 2 | 3 | 4 | 5 | 6 | 7 | 8 | 9 | 10 | A |
|---|---|---|---|---|---|---|---|-----|-----|
| 0 | 0 | 0 | 0 | 0 | 0 | 0 | 0 | +1 | −4 |

denote this running count by TA. When he must make a playing decision he should use the running index corresponding to AC and the strategy tables given at the end of this chapter. When he must make a betting decision he should, first, add AC and TA; then, he should compute

$$\frac{AC + TA}{\text{number of unseen cards}} \qquad (6)$$

The computation of (6) can be done by using one of the methods described in Chapter 5. We observe that (6) *is the running index corresponding to the 99-count. This index should be used for betting decisions.* Of course, the bets should be made according to the betting tables given earlier in this chapter.

Observe that we recommend to the player that he obtain the 99-count by *correcting* the adjusted-count; we did not recommend that he *correct* the 99-count. The reason for this is simple. The player has more time to make betting decisions, than playing decisions. Hence, he should not be required to perform unnecessary calculations before making playing decisions.

The playing strategy can be improved somewhat if, for example, the decisions to split 9s and tens and to double on 9 and 10 are made according to the 99-count strategy.

A count similar to the adjusted-count was introduced in Ref. 19. The count was obtained by *correcting* the complex count.

Instead of the adjusted-count, the player may use the count defined by:

| 2 | 3 | 4 | 5 | 6 | 7 | 8 | 9 | 10 | A |
|----|----|----|----|----|----|----|----|----|----|
| +1 | +2 | +2 | +3 | +2 | +2 | 0 | -1 | -3 | 1 |

$$(7)$$

Observe that the only differences between (5) and (7) are in the weights associated with 2s and 7s. By correcting this count for tens and aces we obtain the count defined by:

| 2 | 3 | 4 | 5 | 6 | 7 | 8 | 9 | 10 | A |
|----|----|----|----|----|----|----|----|----|----|
| +1 | +2 | +2 | +3 | +2 | +2 | 0 | -1 | -2 | -3 |

$$(8)$$

The count defined by (7) is slightly better for playing decisions than the adjusted-count. The 99-count, however, is slightly better for betting than that defined by (8).

### THE 100-COUNT SYSTEM

A slightly better system than that studied in the previous section, is the 100-*count system*. This system is based on the following:

| 2 | 3 | 4 | 5 | 6 | 7 | 8 | 9 | 10 | A |
|----|----|----|------|----|------|----|----|------|----|
| +2 | +2 | +3 | +3.5 | +2 | +1.5 | 0 | -1 | -2.5 | -3 |

On the first line we list the cards and under each card the corresponding number. The 100-count system is, for practical purposes, optimal for betting.

The system is very close to the main system described in *Casino Gambling* (see Ref. 20). Only the numbers associated with the 4s and the 9s are different. In *Casino Gambling* we associated +2.5 with the 4s and –0.5 with the 9s. Here we associate +3 with the 4s and –1 with the 9s.

Since the numbers associated with the 5s, 7s, and tens are not integers, the 100-count system is somewhat more difficult to master than the 99-count system. Of course, the player who has already mastered the system in *Casino Gambling* should not spend time learning a different one.

We observe that we could multiply by 2 the numbers associated with the cards in the above table. The new numbers would now be the integers

$$4, 4, 6, 7, 4, 3, 0, -2, -5, -6$$

However, these numbers are too large. For this, and several other reasons, it is hard to use them in actual play.

For the player who wants to learn the 100-count system, we suggest that he associate with the cards the "symbols"

$$2, 2, 3, 3a, 2, 1a, 0, -1, -2a, -3$$

instead of the numbers

$$2, 2, 3, 3.5, 2, 1.5, 0, -1, -2.5, -3$$

This increases substantially the speed of counting. Of course, 2a+3=5a, 2a+2a=5, 3a+2a=6, etc.

## COMPARISON OF THE BLACKJACK SYSTEMS GIVEN IN THIS BOOK

In this section we shall compare the count systems given in this book.

Below, we order the count systems according to how efficient they are for making betting decisions:

the 100-count;
the 99-count;
the main-count;
the adjusted-count.

The first three counts are excellent for making betting decisions.

In the next list we order the counts according to how efficient they are for making playing decisions:

the adjusted-count;
the main-count;
the 100-count;
the 99-count.

The first two counts are excellent for making playing decisions.

The player who does not *correct* the count he uses might prefer the main-count. This assumes, however, that he will vary the playing strategy according to the count. The player who varies the playing strategy only occasionally, and otherwise uses the basic strategy, might be better off using the 100-count or the 99-count, particularly in multiple-deck games. In general, even experienced gamblers find it easier to vary the betting strategy than the playing strategy. Of course, the player who uses the 99-count for betting decisions and the adjusted-count for playing decisions plays a better game than the players who do not *correct* the counts they use.

THE 99-COUNT SYSTEM
THE APPROXIMATE PLAYING STRATEGY FOR MULTIPLE-DECK GAMES

DRAW STAND (HARD HANDS)

|    | 2    | 3    | 4   | 5   | 6        | 7 | 8 | 9  | 10 | A |
|----|------|------|-----|-----|----------|---|---|----|----|---|
| 17 |      |      |     |     |          |   |   |    |    |   |
| 16 |      |      |     |     |          |   |   | 21 | 1  |   |
| 15 |      |      |     |     |          |   |   |    | 17 |   |
| 14 | −17  | −22  |     |     |          |   |   |    |    |   |
| 13 | −5   | −10  | −16 | −21 | −24/−30  |   |   |    |    |   |
| 12 | 15   | 7    | −1  | −8  | −6/−18   |   |   |    |    |   |

DRAW STAND (SOFT HANDS)
When the dealer's up card is 2, 3, 4, 5, 6, 7 or 8, the player should draw to any soft hand of value 17 or less and stand otherwise. When the dealer's up card is 9 or Ten, the player should draw to any soft hand of value 18 or less and stand otherwise. Assume now the dealer has an Ace up: The player should always draw on 17 or less and stand on 19 or more. When the dealer stands on soft 17, the player should stand on soft 18 if the running index is 6 or more and draw otherwise. When the dealer draws on soft 17, the player should draw on soft 18.

DOUBLING DOWN (HARD HANDS)

|    | 2 | 3 | 4 | 5 | 6 | 7 | 8 | 9 | 10 | A |
|----|---|---|---|---|---|---|---|-----|-----|------|
| 11 |   |   |   |   |   |   |   | −27 | −27 | 4/−4 |
| 10 |   |   |   |   |   |   | −21 | −9 | 16 | 16/12 |
| 9  | 4 | −4 | −13 | −20 |   | 13 |   |   |    |   |
| 8  |   |   | 24 | 16 | 9 |   |   |   |    |   |
| 7  |   |   |   |   |   |   |   |   |    |   |

DOUBLING DOWN (SOFT HANDS)

|    | 2 | 3 | 4 | 5 | 6 | 7 | 8 | 9 | 10 | A |
|----|---|-----|-----|-----|--------|---|---|---|----|---|
| 20 |   |   |   | 20 | 18 |   |   |   |    |   |
| 19 |   | 20 | 11 | 7 | 2/−3 |   |   |   |    |   |
| 18 | 2 | −10 |   |   |   |   |   |   |    |   |
| 17 | 2 | −16 |   |   |   |   |   |   |    |   |
| 16 |   | 12 | −15 |   |   |   |   |   |    |   |
| 15 |   |   | −4 | −26 |   |   |   |   |    |   |
| 14 |   |   | 5 | −14 |   |   |   |   |    |   |
| 13 |   |   | 12 | −2 | −12/−16 |   |   |   |    |   |

SPLITTING (WHEN DOUBLING DOWN AFTER SPLITTING IS NOT ALLOWED)

|      | 2 | 3 | 4 | 5 | 6 | 7 | 8 | 9 | 10 | A |
|------|---|-----|-----|-----|---------|---|---|---|----|-----|
| A, A |   |   |   |   |   |   |   |   |    | −28 |
| T, T |   |   | 25 | 21 | 21 |   |   |   |    |   |
| 9, 9 | −5 | −11 | −16 | −20 | −20/−27 |   |   |   |    | 13/8 |
| 8, 8 |   |   |   |   |   |   |   |   |    |   |
| 7, 7 |   |   |   |   |   |   |   |   |    |   |
| 6, 6 | 6 | −6 | −20 | −25 |   |   |   |   |    |   |
| 5, 5 |   |   |   |   |   |   |   |   |    |   |
| 4, 4 |   |   |   |   |   |   |   |   |    |   |
| 3, 3 |   | 14 | −3 | −15 |   |   |   |   |    |   |
| 2, 2 |   | 10 | −1 | −12 |   |   |   |   |    |   |

## SPLITTING (WHEN DOUBLING DOWN AFTER SPLITTING IS ALLOWED)

| | 2 | 3 | 4 | 5 | 6 | 7 | 8 | 9 | 10 | A |
|---|---|---|---|---|---|---|---|---|---|---|
| A, A | | | | AS IN THE ABOVE TABLE | | | | | | |
| T, T | | | | AS IN THE ABOVE TABLE | | | | | | |
| 9, 9 | −11 | −20 | −25 | | | 15 | | | | 13/7 |
| 8, 8 | | | | | | | | | | |
| 7, 7 | | | | | | | 9 | | | |
| 6, 6 | −11 | −18 | | | | | | | | |
| 5, 5 | | | | | | | | | | |
| 4, 4 | | | 12 | −5 | −15 | | | | | |
| 3, 3 | −7 | | | | | | | | | |
| 2, 2 | −17 | −25 | | | | | 23 | | | |

### SURRENDER

| | 8 | 9 | 10 | A |
|---|---|---|---|---|
| 17 | | | | |
| 16 | 20 | −1 | −13 | −7 |
| 8, 8 | | | 7 | |
| 15 | | 10 | −1 | 5 |
| 14 | | 23 | 14 | 23 |
| 7, 7 | | 20 | 9 | 18 |
| 13 | | | | |

### EARLY SURRENDER

| | 8 | 9 | 10 | A |
|---|---|---|---|---|
| 17 | | | 25 | |
| 16 | 20 | −1 | −25 | |
| 8, 8 | | | −8 | |
| 15 | | 10 | −12 | |
| 14 | | 23 | −2 | |
| 7, 7 | | 20 | −4 | |
| 13 | | | 12 | |
| 12 | | | | |
| 7 | | | | |
| 6 | | | | −20 |
| 5 | | | | 0 |
| 4 | | | | 0 |

### INSURANCE
The player should insure only when the running index is 14 or more

## THE ADJUSTED-COUNT SYSTEM
## THE MULTIPLE-DECK PLAYING STRATEGY

### DRAWING AND STANDING (HARD HANDS)

| | 2 | 3 | 4 | 5 | 6 | 7 | 8 | 9 | 10 | A |
|---|---|---|---|---|---|---|---|---|---|---|
| 17 | | | | | | | | | | −31/−19 |
| 16 | −37 | −43 | −48 | −55 | −50/−60 | 27 | 24 | 20 | 0 | 37/17 |
| 15 | −27 | −34 | −37 | −42 | −40/−50 | 41 | 41 | 35 | 16 | 48/26 |
| 14 | −16 | −21 | −26 | −31 | −31/−37 | 65 | | 57 | 35 | 65/42 |
| 13 | 5 | −10 | −15 | −20 | −20/−25 | | | | | |
| 12 | +13 | 7 | −1 | −7 | −4/−15 | | | | | |

## DRAW STAND (SOFT HANDS)

When the dealer's up card is 2, 3, 4, 5, 6, 7 or 8, the player should draw to any soft hand of value 17 or less and stand otherwise. When the dealer's up card is 9 or Ten, the player should draw to any soft hand of value 18 or less and stand otherwise. Assume now the dealer has an Ace up: The player should always draw on 17 or less and stand on 19 or more. When the dealer stands on soft 17, the player should stand on soft 18 if the running index is 3 or more and draw otherwise. When the dealer draws on soft 17, the player should draw on soft 18.

### DOUBLIND DOWN (HARD HANDS)

|     | 2   | 3   | 4   | 5   | 6   | 7   | 8   | 9   | 10  | A     |
| --- | --- | --- | --- | --- | --- | --- | --- | --- | --- | ----- |
| 11  | −60 | −62 | −65 |     |     | −40 | −30 | −20 | −20 | 2/−1  |
| 10  | −52 | −56 | −62 | −65 | −75 | −32 | −24 | −10 | 20  | 20/15 |
| 9   | 5   | −4  | −13 | −21 | −31 | 14  | 33  |     |     |       |
| 8   | 60  | 40  | 25  | 17  | 10  | 65  |     |     |     |       |
| 7   |     |     | 65  | 50  | 50  |     |     |     |     |       |

### DOUBLING DOWN (SOFT HANDS)

|     | 2   | 3   | 4   | 5   | 6       | 7   | 8   | 9   | 10  | A   |
| --- | --- | --- | --- | --- | ------- | --- | --- | --- | --- | --- |
| 20  | 47  | 41  | 35  | 27  | 24      |     |     |     |     |     |
| 19  | 41  | 23  | 15  | 12  | 4/−1    |     |     |     |     |     |
| 18  | 4   | −4  | −25 | −35 | −37/−55 |     |     |     |     |     |
| 17  | 4   | −12 | −28 | −44 | −60     |     |     |     |     |     |
| 16  |     | 12  | −1  | −25 | −50     |     |     |     |     |     |
| 15  |     | 17  | 0   | −17 | −35     |     |     |     |     |     |
| 14  | 44  | 23  | 6   | −14 | −21     |     |     |     |     |     |
| 13  | 38  | 23  | +10 | −2  | −11     |     |     |     |     |     |

### SPLIT (WHEN DOUBLING DOWN AFTER SPLITTING IS NOT ALLOWED)

|      | 2   | 3   | 4   | 5   | 6       | 7   | 8   | 9   | 10   | A     |
| ---- | --- | --- | --- | --- | ------- | --- | --- | --- | ---- | ----- |
| A, A | −53 | −53 | −53 |     |         | −41 | −40 | −35 | −34  | −17   |
| T, T | 50  | 40  | 32  | 22  | 22      |     |     |     |      |       |
| 9, 9 | −6  | −12 | −18 | −24 | −20/−26 |     |     |     |      | 30/25 |
| 8, 8 |     |     |     |     |         |     |     |     | 27●  |       |
| 7, 7 | −50 | −50 |     |     |         |     |     |     |      |       |
| 6, 6 | 6   | −6  | −19 | −27 | −35     |     |     |     |      |       |
| 5, 5 |     |     |     |     |         |     |     |     |      |       |
| 4, 4 |     |     |     |     |         |     |     |     |      |       |
| 3, 3 |     | 14  | −3  | −16 |         | 39● |     |     |      |       |
| 2, 2 | 33  | 12  | −1  | −13 |         |     |     |     |      |       |

### SPLITTING (WHEN DOUBLING DOWN AFTER SPLITTING IS ALLOWED)

|      | 2   | 3   | 4   | 5   | 6        | 7  | 8 | 9 | 10 |       |
|------|-----|-----|-----|-----|----------|----|---|---|----|-------|
| A, A | AS IN THE ABOVE TABLE |||||||||        |
| T, T | AS IN THE ABOVE TABLE |||||||||        |
| 9, 9 | −9  | −20 | −25 | −32 | −32/−38  | 20 |   |   |    | 19/14 |
| 8, 8 |     |     |     |     |          |    |   |   | 40• |       |
| 7, 7 | −50 | −50 |     |     |          |    | 4 |   |    |       |
| 6, 6 | −15 | −23 | −28 | −38 |          |    |   |   |    |       |
| 5, 5 |     |     |     |     |          |    |   |   |    |       |
| 4, 4 |     | 40  | 20  | 3   | 2        |    |   |   |    |       |
| 3, 3 | −12 | −38 |     |     |          |    |   |   |    |       |
| 2, 2 | −18 | −25 | −27 | −35 |          |    |   |   |    |       |

### SURRENDER

|      | 8  | 9   | 10  | A  |
|------|----|-----|-----|----|
| 17   |    | 50  | 50  |    |
| 16   | 31 | −1  | −10 | −2 |
| 8, 8 |    | 38  | 9   |    |
| 15   | 40 | 12  | −1  | 9  |
| 14   | 45 | 29  | 17  | 29 |
| 7, 7 | 41 | 20  | 11  | 17 |
| 13   |    | 50  | 38  | 50 |

### EARLY SURRENDER

|      | 8  | 9   | 10  | A   |
|------|----|-----|-----|-----|
| 17   |    | 50  | 40  |     |
| 16   | 31 | −1  | −30 |     |
| 8, 8 |    | 38  | −10 |     |
| 15   | 40 | 12  | −20 |     |
| 14   | 45 | 29  | −4  |     |
| 7, 7 | 41 | 20  | −6  |     |
| 13   |    | 50  | 17  |     |
| 12   |    |     | 35  | −35 |
| 7    |    |     |     | −30 |
| 6    |    |     |     | −20 |
| 5    |    |     |     | 1   |
| 4    |    |     |     | 2   |

INSURANCE
The player should insure only when the running index is 13 or more

# 5
# Miscellany

The main parts of this chapter are the first four sections.

In the first one we discuss betting procedures and we indicate what capital the player should have.

In the second section we give a short list of casinos and corresponding blackjack rules.

The first two sections also contains various remarks which, directly or indirectly, suggest how the player should conduct himself in a casino.

In the third section we suggest how the player should practice. It is essential, in our opinion, that one practice with a large number of decks shuffled together and not with a single deck.

In the fourth section we give methods for the computation of the running index in actual games. This index is almost impossible to compute directly. Various authors prefer true indices (see the third subsection). We prefer to use running indices and we compute them by using the *Second method*. In actual games, we do not like to perform divisions by numbers larger than 2 (except for divisions by 10) and we do not like to estimate visually the number of unseen cards.

## GENERAL REMARKS RELATED
## TO BETTING

As we have already written, if one plays blackjack skillfully, for example, if one uses one of the winning systems described in this book, he will have an advantage over the house. The advantage, however, is not very large. The reader should also realize that in blackjack one does not have on every deal a probability greater than 1/2 of winning the corresponding hand. For these, and other reasons, the fluctuations in player's capital might be quite large. Only in the long run may one get substantially ahead.

To win, the player must have substantial capital, time to play long enough, and nerves of steel.

The playing strategy should be followed strictly. The player who lost ten successive hands by drawing to a stiff against high cards should draw again if the playing strategy recommends it.

Certain authors suggest that blackjack players should make, sometimes, incorrect playing decisions with the purpose of confusing the casino personnel watching them. Although we do not like this method we must recognize that it has a certain usefulness. In any case it should be used only in exceptional situations. It would be best, of course, if one could make a play which appeared to be wrong but which, in fact, was the right one.

For various reasons, it is much more important to disguise the betting strategy. Before we discuss this matter further, we shall make several remarks concerning the betting tables given in Chapters 3 and 4 for the main-count and the 99-count systems.

These tables recommend, within certain approximations, that when the player has an $\alpha\%$ advantage the bet should be "a multiple of $\alpha$." This means that there is a $\lambda > 0$ such that when the player's advantage is $\alpha\%$ the bet should be

$$\beta = \lambda\alpha \tag{9}$$

The betting strategy would be in fact, more precise if, instead of using the tables mentioned above, the bets would be determined directly on the basis of (9). The choice of $\lambda$ depends, among other things, on the player's total capital and on the betting limits offered at the table where the game takes place. In this book

$$\lambda = \frac{\text{player's capital}}{100}$$

From the betting tables we deduce that the player's capital should be about 800 units.

The player's capital changes continuously during the game. It increases when he wins and decreases when he loses. Strictly speaking, the betting unit should be increased when the capital increases and decreased when it decreases. It is almost impossible for a player to correctly modify the betting unit during the game. The betting unit must be chosen before the start of the playing session.

We observe that the player is in danger of being quickly ruined if his betting unit is too large in relation to his capital.

The betting tables in Chapters 3 and 4 give excellent strategies. Nevertheless, for various reasons which we discuss below, the player might be unable to use these tables exactly as they are written. In such cases the tables should guide only the player's strategies.

The running index may change drastically from one round of play, to the next one, even in multiple-deck play. It might indicate a 1-unit bet on the first round and a 6-unit bet on the second one. If one changes the bet too often and too much, his play will be scrutinized by the dealer, by the pit boss, etc. Bet variation is one of the characteristics of skillful play and casino managements are aware of it. It is natural for them not to like skillful players. After all casinos are built for profit. Of course, there is nothing special about this; every business enterprise has the same goal. What might be unexpected, for the uninformed reader, is that casinos often take countermeasures against skillful players and sometimes bar them from further play. This is, of course, "very interesting." The players are offered all kinds of options in the game of blackjack. They are told that they can exercise these options any way they wish. Nevertheless, if they exercise the options well, on the basis of the information furnished by the house, they become undesirables.

Even "more interesting" is the attitude of certain gaming commissions. Instead of "investigating so thoroughly" the background of casino owners it would be better if these commissions would make certain that: 1) the games are dealt honestly, everywhere; 2) no steps are taken to discourage players because they are winning and no civilized patron, skillful or not, is bothered in any way.

In any case, until these matters are settled, the player should be aware that it is not in his interest to advertise that he knows what he is doing at a blackjack table. Unfortunately, no matter what the player does, it is doubtful that he will be able to disguise, very much, his play.

It is very interesting to observe that many of the authors who recommend various methods for hiding skillful play say that they, themselves, were barred. Nevertheless, there is a "fool-proof" method one can use to make certain that one will never be barred. The method is the following: The player should learn perfectly a winning system. Then, in actual games he should do exactly the opposite of what the system recommends and he should make certain that he always loses. This way nobody will ever know that he is skillful. Such methods have been already recommended in the blackjack literature.

Although the player cannot win in usual multiple-deck games without increasing the bet in favorable situations, sudden and large bet variations should be avoided.*

A relatively smooth method of betting is the following: The player should start by betting 1 unit. As soon as the running index indicates** a bet of 2 units or more he should bet 2 units. Assume that he wins this bet. Then there will be 4 units in his betting area: The initial bet plus the payoff for the win. The player should bet now as the running index indicates, *but no more than 4 units.* If he lost the 2-unit bet he should, again, bet as the running index indicates but *should not increase his bet.* The player should proceed in the same manner after winning or losing a 4-unit or 8-unit bet.

Whether the player should increase his bet to 12 units, depends on the conditions in the casino he is playing and on his personality. No general rule can be given. One should realize, however, that the more he bets in favorable situations the greater will be his gain.

The following example helps us understand the above method: Consider a player who participates in a four-deck game and uses the main-count and Table 1 in Chapter 3. Assume that he bets 1 unit "on this round of play" and that, at the beginning of the next five rounds the running indices are, respectively,

$$+5, +7, +16, +3, +11.$$

In this case the player bets 2 units, 4 units (if he has won the previous bet), 8 units (if he has won the previous bet), 1 unit, 2 units. If the running indices were

$$+5, +11, +16, +9, +30,$$

---

*The player *cannot win* by betting only 1 or 2 units.
**Of course "the decisions" are taken by comparing the running index with the "critical index" in the corresponding betting table.

he would have bet 2 units, 4 units (if he had won the previous bet), 8 units (if he had won the previous bet), 4 units, 8 units (if he had won the previous bet). The player should not increase his bet to more than 2 units after a loss.

In exceptional cases the player may bet 12 units after betting 2. For example, assume that one bet 2 units and was dealt (8, 8). He split the pair and received a 3 on the first 8; he doubled down on (8, 3). He received a ten on the other 8. If he wins with both hands there will be a total of 12 units in his betting area. If the running index indicates a 12 unit bet he can bet the total amount if he thinks that he can get away with it.

A method of betting, less conservative than the one described above, is the following: The player should start by betting 1 unit. As soon as the running index indicates a bet of 2 or more units he should bet 2 units. As long as the running index indicates a bet of 2 or more units *he should now increase the bet in case of a win (according to the scale 2, 4, 8, 12) and leave it unchanged in case of a loss.*

It would be ideal for the player to bet only in favorable situations (see Ref. 51). In our opinion this is very difficult; in multiple-deck games it is almost impossible. A shoe rarely becomes favorable very quickly. Also, one cannot get in and out of a game all the time. Nevertheless, we observe that if one makes ten $1,000 bets when he has an advantage of 1% or more, he will make, on the average, more than $100.

There are players who, on various pretexts, leave multiple-deck games when the running index becomes too low, ask the dealer to hold their chair and return when the cards are being shuffled.

A somewhat related "scheme" is the following: A player plants associates at several tables in the same casino. These associates bet low and signal when "the shoe becomes favorable" at their table. The player walks from table to table, and places high bets when his associates signal him to do so. This method was popularized by K. Uston (Ref. 47).

We conclude by observing that to win a substantial amount one must bet substantial amounts. Roughly speaking, when the bet unit is $5, one cannot make more than about $65 in about eight hours of play. Whether this is enough, is for the player to decide.

## CASINOS, GAMES AND RULES

As we have already said, the player's expectation and strategies depend on the rules under which the game is played. The player should learn therefore, before or soon after he starts playing, what the rules are.

Some casinos publish pamphlets describing the games they offer. Nevertheless, these pamphlets rarely state precisely the rules under which the blackjack games are played.

Of course, the player may ask the dealer what the rules are. Nevertheless, this should be done rarely, and when it is, the inquiry should appear casual. Some of the dealers, pit bosses, etc., seem to believe that anybody who asks "whether two aces can be split" is a skillful player, and naturally, they do not like such players. The player who asks details about the rules attracts unnecessary attention. Under present casino conditions this should be avoided.

To publish a complete and correct list of casinos and corresponding blackjack rules is almost impossible. One of the reasons for this difficulty is that rules often change. In any case, for the reader's general orientation we give below several indications.

On the Las Vegas strip the blackjack games are played, generally, under the basic rules. There are, however, many exceptions. Several casinos offer the important options of doubling down after splitting and surrendering (Caesars Palace, for example, offers both these options).

In casinos in downtown Las Vegas the games are played, generally, under basic rules, except that, in most places, the dealer draws to soft 17.

In casinos in the Reno–Tahoe area, the Reno–Tahoe rules are offered.

The Eastern rules were offered in Atlantic City. Recently, the early surrender option, the main attraction of the eastern rules, was eliminated.

The British rules are encountered in casinos in Great Britain.

In the Bahamas, the games are played under basic rules, except that doubling down is allowed only on hard hands having the values 9, 10, or 11. In Aruba, the games are no hole-card games of type I (English style), the dealer draws to soft 17 and the player can double only on hard 10 and hard 11.

In Las Vegas, single-deck and multiple-deck blackjack games are offered. In the Reno-Tahoe area most games are dealt from a single deck. The other games mentioned above are dealt from multiple-deck packs.

When the player does not know exactly the rules offered in the casino he is playing in, he should try to exercise the options which are most favorable for him. For instance, if he holds (9, 7) against a dealer's 10 he should try to surrender, if his playing strategy recommends it. If the casino does not allow surrender the dealer will inform him. This way, the player will learn whether the option is offered. The main problem when proceeding in this manner is related to splitting pairs. For example, assume that a basic strategy player is dealt a (2, 2); the dealer has a 2 up. The basic strategy recommends the splitting of (2, 2) only when the option of doubling after splitting is offered. Assume that the player does not know if this option can be exercised. What should he do? In such situations we proceed conservatively. We do not split until we learn whether we can double down after splitting.

As we have said many times in this book, we prefer, by far, the four-deck games, although it is true that, theoretically, single-deck games are more favorable for the player than multiple-deck games (when they are dealt under the same rules and conditions). Nevertheless, we rarely participate in games in which the dealer holds the cards in his hand. There are many reasons for this; most have been mentioned earlier in this book. Games dealt from more than four decks should be avoided, unless the rules and the corresponding playing conditions are exceptionally favorable.

For the skillful player, it is preferable that the cards be dealt face up. In this case he can see more cards before he makes his playing decisions. Also, for various reasons, the probability of making counting mistakes increases when the cards are dealt face down.

In general, the player should not enter a game unless "the conditions seem favorable." Some reasons why the conditions might not be favorable are listed below:

1. The rules are bad, or very bad.
2. The dealer "inserts the joker very high;" hence, a substantial

part of the pack of cards used in the game is not dealt. In general the player should avoid four-deck games in which "the joker is inserted higher than 90 cards from the end."

3. The dealer is unpleasant.
4. The game is conducted in disorderly manner.
5. The desired seats are occupied.

As far as unpleasant dealers are concerned, we observe that a player should not continue to play in such a situation so that he shows the dealer, the pit boss, etc., who is "the smarter." If he, the player, is "the smarter," then he should change tables or even casinos.

As far as seats are concerned, we observe that we do not play at a full table unless we can sit either on the last chair to the dealer's right or on the adjacent one. In fact, we prefer the second position since from there we can see better the cards on the table. Also, from these positions we do not have to move our eyes too much when looking at the cards on the table. In any case, we do not sit at a table if more than one hand is played on our left. And, we do not move from the chair we selected if some "smart" player who wants to play two hands, for example, asks us to. We simply say that the chair we are sitting on is our "lucky chair." We suggest, politely, that the "smart" player goes . . . somewhere else.

It is also advisable to avoid tables where bad players are gambling. This is, however, almost impossible. Even the basic strategy is known by very few persons. On the other hand, bad blackjack players do not affect, *in the long run,* other players expectations. The following true story helps us to understand why: "A little one, honey," asks the player who sat on my left and who holds (10, 4). This is of course a very bad play. The dealer has a 6 up and many tens remain unseen. And "honey" busts the player with a big jack. The dealer's hole card is a 9. Hence, the jack would have busted her. Instead, she draws a 4, which gives her a total of 19. Everybody at the table loses on this round, due to the bad draw of our player. But imagine that the next two cards would have been *a 4 and a jack,* instead of *a jack and a 4.* In this case, by drawing to (10, 4) against a 6, our player would have caused the dealer to bust. Observe now that the orderings of the next two cards, mentioned above, are equally likely to occur. It follows that the manner in which the player on my left proceeds does not make any difference, in the long run, to anyone, except himself.

Bad players are, of course, irritating. Nevertheless, we must learn to put up with them. They are more of a threat to the sanity of skillful players than to their bankroll.

## HOW TO PRACTICE

As soon as the player can remember the weights of the cards, he should start practicing with an eight-deck pack. Beginners should count slowly, very slowly if necessary, and try not to make mistakes. Of course, the player should be able to count fast enough before playing in a casino game. One should be able to count a single deck in about 30 seconds and an eight-deck pack in about 4 minutes.

The players who practice at home with a single deck and then have difficulties in four-deck casino games should not be surprised. In four-deck games, the running counts often become much larger or much smaller than in single-deck games. This is one of the reasons why counting in multiple-deck games is somewhat harder. During practice, I often start with a running count of –10, –20, +10 or +20. This way, I have a better chance of encountering very large and very small running counts. Many players find more difficult the handling of negative counts than of positive counts. These players should practice more often with negative running counts.

It takes time to learn to keep track of the cards dealt at a blackjack table. *Although everybody who knows how to add and subtract can learn to count perfectly, only a few will make the necessary effort to succeed.* Learning one of the blackjack systems described in this book does not require any special talent. It requires will!

The player should practice counting every day, even during periods when not playing in casinos. For at least a week before participating in actual games the training should be more intense.

One may practice when walking on the street, riding a train, etc. It is not necessary to carry a deck of cards for this. One should identify every "0" he sees with a ten, every "1" with an ace, every "2" with a 2, every "3" with a 3, etc. In general, the running counts become quickly positive and large, when practicing in this manner. For this reason, it is preferable to start from –50 and count until the running counts become about +50. Then, one should start all over again.

When a complete eight-deck pack is counted, the running counts and $N$ ($N$ = the number of unseen cards) should be zero, at the end of the pack. When they are not, mistakes were made. To estimate the progress in learning to count the cards, the player should average the "absolute values" of these errors over every *one hundred eight-deck packs*. Of course, the better one counts, the smaller these averages will be.

It is most unfortunate when a player believes he can count accurately, when in fact, he cannot. This player will have costly and discouraging experiences.

Even good players may count badly in certain circumstances. For example:

The good player, who plays when he is tired, will probably make mistakes. Of course, it does not matter if he is tired since he has played already for six hours, or since he has just arrived in Las Vegas from Kalamazoo, Michigan.

The good player, who has many things on his mind and who thinks of his personal problems, instead of the game, will almost certainly play badly. The player should concentrate on the game and forget everything else while playing.

The good player, who has won in the last several sessions, might become overconfident and careless, and hence, start making mistakes. The inevitable substantial loss will bring this player back to reality.

The tennis player who participates in a tournament should, and probably will, continue to play even after he realizes that he is not in good form. The blackjack player does not need to gamble when he has a bad day, intellectually or physically.

The various strategy tables, corresponding to the system the player desires to use, should be learned by heart. Although this might seem a difficult task, one should not get discouraged.

The player should first learn the tables giving the approximate playing strategy and one or two of the betting tables. He should start with the tables giving the strategies for drawing and standing and for doubling down on hard hands. At this stage, the other decisions should be made according to the basic strategy.

For a certain period of time, the player should read the tables several times, every day. One learns this way easily, without too much effort and without spending more than a few minutes per day. The player should continue to study the tables even after *mastering* the playing and betting strategies. Otherwise he will forget what he has learned. He should read the tables before every playing session.

The player should be able to recall *instantly* the necessary critical indices. For example, the player who uses the main-count system and holds (5, 2, 6) against a 3, should remember *instantly* that he must stand if the running index is –8 or more, and draw otherwise. The player who uses the 99-count system and holds (5, 5) against a king, should remember instantly that he must double down if the running index is 16 or more, and draw otherwise.

The players who do not want to learn a winning method of play, should at least study the basic strategy. Otherwise, their play will be very poor.

Various advertisers promise to teach the player winning blackjack strategies in several hours. The systems they advertise are, of course, "the greatest".* From the stories these advertisers tell it seems that, when they play, they never lose one hand! When they draw to hard 16, they get, of course, a 5. When they stand on 12, the dealer busts. I assume that when they double down on 7 they get, somehow, "a 14." Their students are led to believe that if they ever need a pair of shoes, all they have to do is find a casino, any casino, and play a few hands of blackjack. These claims are ridiculous. Nevertheless, since they are very often repeated, they are taken seriously, sometimes, even by casino managements. It would be a waste of time to comment further on these matters.

---

*The usual method is to say that X, Y, and Z won substantially by using their systems. Of course, they omit to mention the hundreds or thousands of players who lost. The same method is used by "your broker," when recommending an investment, by "your senator," etc. The saddest part of all this is that many of these persons do not realize that they are talking nonsense.

## HOW TO COMPUTE THE RUNNING INDEX

As we stated above, it is quite difficult to compute the running index directly during actual play. In this section, we give two methods which can be used to determine this index, within a certain approximation. These methods are based on Tables 1 and 2. In writing these tables we have taken into account, among other things, the basic strategy and the fact that in single-deck games most of the hands are dealt, not from the middle of the deck, but from the upper half. The first method is the easiest to use. The second one gives a more precise evaluation of the running index. We use the second method in actual games. In the last part of the section we discuss true indices.

To compute the running index we must know, at each moment of play, the number of *unseen* cards. We may determine this number by counting the cards as they are dealt and seen. For example, assume that the game is played with a four-deck pack. The total number of cards in the pack is 208. Each time a card is dealt and seen, we subtract 1. When we have seen 42 cards, the number of unseen cards is

$$208-42 = 166$$

If, at this moment, the running count is 12, the running index is

$$\frac{12 \times 100}{166} = \frac{1200}{166} = \text{about } 7$$

*It is important to remember that we count only the cards we can see.* The number of cards remaining in the pack used in the game is not necessarily the same as the number of unseen cards.

When the number $N$, of unseen cards, is between 101 and 200 ($101 \leqslant N \leqslant 200$) we find it easier to keep track of $N-100$ instead of $N$. Of course, to determine the running index corresponding to a running count, we divide by $N$ and not by $N-100$.

More precisely, in a four-deck game we start from "a total number of cards equal to 8 and then from a total number of cards equal to 100." Once we have seen 108 cards we start again from "100." A similar method can be used in games dealt from more than 4 decks.

*Example.* — Assume that we play in a four-deck game and that we use the main-count system. The first seven cards we see are

5, 5, king, 8, 6, jack, 7.

The corresponding running count is 3. The number of unseen cards "is indicated by 1 (8 – 7 = 1)." If the next card we see is a 2, the running count becomes 4, and the number of unseen cards "is indicated by 100." Hence, at this moment, the number of unseen cards is 200. If the next two cards we see are a 5 and an ace, the running count becomes 5, and the number of unseen cards "is indicated by 98." Hence, at this moment, the number of unseen cards is 198.

Instead of counting *backwards* each card he sees, the player may try to *estimate visually the number of unseen cards.* If he is confident that his estimation is reasonably accurate, he may use it for computing the running index. This method is used by a few successful players and by many others, who pretend to be successful.

Instead of counting backwards, the player may count *forwards* the cards he sees. In this case the tables giving the values of the running index must be modified. We count backwards, since we prefer to use a parameter which decreases instead of one which increases.

### The First Method

This method uses Table 1.* To explain how the table should be read, we start by noticing that the numbers to the left of the arrows (denoted $x$) are *running counts,* while those to the right of the arrows are *running indices*:

---

*For every number $x$, $x/2$ is one half of $x$, $x/3$ is one third of $x$, etc.

**Table 1**

| | | |
|---:|:---:|:---|
| $261,312{:}x$ | $\rightarrow$ | $(3x)/10$ |
| $209,260{:}x$ | $\rightarrow$ | $(4x)/10$ |
| $157,208{:}x$ | $\rightarrow$ | $x/2$ |
| $105,156{:}x$ | $\rightarrow$ | $2(x/3)$ |
| $53,104{:}x$ | $\rightarrow$ | $x$ |
| $27,52{:}x$ | $\rightarrow$ | $2x$ |
| $1,26{:}x$ | $\rightarrow$ | $4x$ |

The player who decides to use this table, particularly if he estimates visually the number of unseen cards, should remember that:

> a six-deck pack contains 312 cards;
> a five-deck pack contains 260 cards;
> a four-deck pack contains 208 cards;
> a three-deck pack contains 156 cards;
> a two-deck pack contains 104 cards.

*Let $N$ be the number of unseen cards.* If, for example, $N$ is between 157 and 208 ($157 \leqslant N \leqslant 208$) and the running count is 12, we use the row

$$157,208{:}x \quad \rightarrow \quad x/2$$

of Table 1, and obtain the running index

$$12/2 = 6.$$

If $N$ is between 105 and 156 and the running count is 16, we use the row

$$105,156{:}x \quad \rightarrow \quad 2(x/3)$$

of Table 1, and obtain the running index

$$2 \times (16/3) = \text{about } 11.$$

If $N = 47$ and the running index is 5 we use the row

$$27, 52{:}x \quad \rightarrow \quad 2x$$

of Table 1, and obtain the running index

$$2 \times 5 = 10.$$

The running index is determined in the same manner when the running count is *negative*. For example, if $N = 145$ and the running count is –25, we use the row

$$105, 156{:}x \quad \rightarrow \quad 2(x/3)$$

of Table 1, and obtain the running index

$$2 \times (-25/3) = \text{about } -17.$$

We obtain the same result if we compute first the running index corresponding to 25 and then, multiply by –1.

If we play in an eight-deck game, if $313 \leqslant N \leqslant 416$ and if $x$ is the running count, $2x/10$ is a good estimation of the running index.

Instead of adjusting the running counts, according to the number of unseen cards, one could adjust the indices in the betting and strategy tables. Hence, instead of computing running indices, one would multiply the indices in the betting and strategy tables. In theory, this might seem easier, particularly if one would write the tables differently. In practice, this would probably be even more difficult than computing running indices.

### The Second Method

This method is a variant of *The first method*, and uses Table 2. The table is read, essentially, in the same manner as Table 1. Observe that for certain values of $N$ (recall that $N$ is the number of unseen cards)

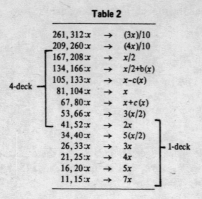

**Table 2**

| | | |
|---|---|---|
| 261, 312 :x | → | (3x)/10 |
| 209, 260 :x | → | (4x)/10 |
| 167, 208 :x | → | x/2 |
| 134, 166 :x | → | x/2+b(x) |
| 105, 133 :x | → | x−c(x) |
| 81, 104 :x | → | x |
| 67, 80 :x | → | x+c(x) |
| 53, 66 :x | → | 3(x/2) |
| 41, 52 :x | → | 2x |
| 34, 40 :x | → | 5(x/2) |
| 26, 33 :x | → | 3x |
| 21, 25 :x | → | 4x |
| 16, 20 :x | → | 5x |
| 11, 15 :x | → | 7x |

4-deck bracket covers rows 167,208 through 41,52. 1-deck bracket covers rows 34,40 through 11,15.

the computation of the running index corresponding to $x$ uses the *corrections* $b(x)$ and $c(x)$. We must therefore explain what these corrections are. This is done in Table 3, which is read as follows: When the *running count* $x$ is between two of the numbers in the first column, on the same row, the corrections $b(x)$ and $c(x)$ are given in the second and third column, respectively. For example,

**Table 3**

| $x$ | $b(x)$ | $c(x)$ |
|---|---|---|
| 11, 15 | 1 | 3 |
| 16, 19 | 1 | 4 |
| 20, 29 | 2 | 6 |
| 30, 39 | 3 | 8 |
| 40, 49 | 4 | 11 |
| 50, 59 | 5 | 14 |
| 60, 69 | 6 | 16 |

if $x$ is between 20 and 29, $b(x) = 2$ and $c(x) = 6$. If $x$ is between 40 and 49, $b(x) = 4$ and $c(x) = 11$. If $x = 17$, $b(x) = 1$ and $c(x) = 4$.*

It is easy to remember the values of the correction $b$, if we observe that they are equal to the first digits of the numbers in the first column.

---

*Notice that we defined $b(x)$ and $c(x)$ only for values of $x$ between 11 and 69. As we shall see below, this is enough for our purpose.

The introduction of the corrections $b$ and $c$ facilitates and speeds the computation of the running index, in actual games. The idea of using these corrections is due, essentially, to Simon Carruthers.

*The following examples should further clarify the computation of the running index.*

If $N$ is between 67 and 80, and the running count is 17, we use the row

$$67, 80 : x \quad \rightarrow \quad x + c(x)$$

of Table 2, and obtain the running index

$$17 + c(17) = 17 + 4 = 21.$$

If $N$ is between 134 and 166, and the running count is 24, we use the row

$$134, 166 : x \quad \rightarrow \quad x/2 + b(x)$$

of Table 2, and obtain the running index

$$24/2 + b(24) = 12 + 2 = 14.$$

*If the running count is negative, for example -18, we compute first the running index corresponding to 18 and then, we multiply by -1.* If, for instance, $N$ is between 134 and 166, the running index corresponding to 18 is

$$18/2 + b(18) = 9 + 1 = 10.$$

Therefore, the running index corresponding to -18 is -10.

When we must divide by 2 and when the division cannot be performed exactly, we replace $x$ by $x + 1$, if $N$ is greater than 100 and by $x - 1$, if $N$ is less than 100. For example, if $n = 160$ and the running count is -25, we calculate first the running index corresponding to 25. We obtain

$$(26/2) + 2 = 15.$$

We conclude that the running index corresponding to –25 is –15.

Observe that Table 3 does not define the values of the corrections $b$ and $c$, for running counts between 1 and 10. In actual blackjack games we use Table 4, to determine the running index, when the running count is between –10 and +10 and $N$ is between the numbers listed in the first column. For other values of $N$, we use Table 2, no matter what the running count is. For instance, if $N$ is between 67 and 80 and the running count is 7, the running index is 9. If $N$ is between 105 and 133 and the running count is –6, the running index is –8. If $N$ is between 34 and 40 and the running count is 9, the running index is 22. If $N$ is between 167 and 208 and the running count is –5, the running index is –3.

**Table 4**

|          | 1 | 2 | 3 | 4 | 5 | 6 | 7 | 8 | 9 | 10 |
|----------|---|---|---|---|---|---|---|---|---|----|
| 134, 166 | 1 | 1 | 2 | 2 | 3 | 4 | 4 | 5 | 5 | 6 |
| 105, 133 | 1 | 2 | 2 | 3 | 4 | 4 | 5 | 6 | 7 | 8 |
| 67, 80   | 1 | 2 | 4 | 5 | 6 | 8 | 9 | 10 | 11 | 12 |
| 53, 66   | 1 | 3 | 5 | 6 | 8 | 9 | 11 | 12 | 13 | 15 |
| 34, 40   | 2 | 5 | 7 | 10 | 12 | 15 | 18 | 20 | 22 | 25 |

The running index is obviously zero, when the running count is zero.

### True Indices

The *true index* is

$$\frac{\text{running count} \times 52}{\text{number of unseen cards}} \tag{10}$$

It is obvious that the *true index* is about half the running index.

In Chapters 3 and 4, we expressed the betting and playing decisions a player has to make in terms of running indices. These decisions can be also expressed in terms of true indices. For example, assume that a player who uses the main-count system has hard 12 and that the dealer's up card is a 2. The player should stand if the running count is 9 or more. We deduce that the player should stand if the true index is 5 or more.

The *true index* can be determined using Table 5. Although written somewhat differently, this table should be read in the same way as Tables 1 and 2 were. As in Tables 1 and 2, the values to the left of the arrows are running counts. Those to the right of the arrows are true indices. A row as

**Table 5**

| | | |
|---|---|---|
| 5D, 6D: $x$ | $\rightarrow$ | $x/6$ |
| 4D, 5D: $x$ | $\rightarrow$ | $x/5$ |
| 3½D, 4D: $x$ | $\rightarrow$ | $x/4$ |
| 3D, 3½D: $x$ | $\rightarrow$ | $(2x)/7$ |
| 2½D, 3D: $x$ | $\rightarrow$ | $x/3$ |
| 2D, 2½D: $x$ | $\rightarrow$ | $(2x)/5$ |
| 1½D, 2D: $x$ | $\rightarrow$ | $2x$ |
| 1D, 1½D: $x$ | $\rightarrow$ | $(2x)/3$ |
| ¾D, 1D: $x$ | $\rightarrow$ | $x$ |
| ½D, ¾D: $x$ | $\rightarrow$ | $(4x)/3$ |
| ¼D, ½D: $x$ | $\rightarrow$ | $2x$ |
| 0D ¼D: $x$ | $\rightarrow$ | $4x$ |

$$3D, 3½D: x \quad \rightarrow \quad (2x)/7$$

should be read as follows: If the number $N$, of unseen cards, is between 156 (156 is the number of cards in a usual 3-deck pack) and 182 (182 is the number of cards in 3½-deck pack) and the running count is $x$, the true index is $(2x)/7$. For example, if $N = 160$ and $x = 17$, Table 5 gives the true index

$$(2 \times 17)/7 = 34/7 = \text{about } 4.85$$

In an actual play we would use the value 5. Observe that the exact true index is 5.52.

One other *true index* encountered in the blackjack literature is

$$\frac{\text{running count} \times 26}{\text{number of unseen cards}} \quad (11)$$

This *index* is about one fourth of the *running index*.

The indices (1) and (2) are usually called *true counts* (see Ref. 27, 38, and 48).

*For various reasons we prefer to use the running index and the second method for computing it.*

**Practice Table**

Table 6 was prepared for the player who participates in four-deck games and who uses the second method for computing the running indices. The table should be used as follows: The player starts by reading the first row. This row contains the numbers 3 and 150. The first one is assumed to be the *running count;* the second one, the number of *unseen cards.* The player should compute the corresponding *running index.* Then, he should read the other rows and proceed in the same manner.

**Table 6**

| RUNNING COUNTS | UNSEEN CARDS | RUNNING INDICES |
|:---:|:---:|:---:|
| 3 | 150 | ? |
| 6 | 139 | ? |
| 5 | 65 | ? |
| 3 | 65 | ? |
| 25 | 145 | ? |
| 25 | 117 | ? |
| 23 | 77 | ? |
| 25 | 60 | ? |
| 35 | 148 | ? |
| 35 | 115 | ? |
| 36 | 70 | ? |
| 36 | 65 | ? |
| 40 | 166 | ? |
| 41 | 120 | ? |
| 40 | 80 | ? |
| 43 | 66 | ? |

## RUNNING COUNTS OF CERTAIN
## GROUPS OF CARDS

The players who decide to study one of the methods of play given in this book, should learn by heart the running counts corresponding

to certain groups of cards. This will facilitate and speed considerably
the counting process. For example, the player who uses the 99-count
and sees a 5, a ten, and a 9 should realize immediately that the corresponding running count is zero (indeed, +3 + (-2) + (-1) = 0).

Below, we give a few examples. They were suggested by players
using the systems given in this book.

*Examples corresponding to the main-count:*

| Group of cards | Running count |
|---|---|
| (10, 4), (10, 5), (10, 6) | 0 |
| (10, 2), (10, 3), (10, 7) | -1 |
| (A, 2), (A, 3), (A, 7) | 0 |
| (A, 4), (A, 5), (A, 6) | +1 |
| (10, 10, A) | -5 |
| (10, 2, 3), (10, 2, 7), (10, 3, 7), etc. | 0 |
| (10, 10, 4, 4), (10, 10, 4, 5), (10, 10, 4, 6), etc. | 0 |

*Examples corresponding to the 99-count:*

| Group of cards | Running count |
|---|---|
| (10, 7) | -1 |
| (10, 5) | +1 |
| (10, 2), (10, 3), (10, 4), (10, 6) | 0 |
| (9, 7) | 0 |
| (10, 9, 5) | 0 |
| (10, A, 5) | -2 |
| (10, A, 7) | -4 |
| (10, 10, 2, 2), (10, 10, 2, 3), (10, 10, 2, 4), etc. | 0 |

*Examples corresponding to the 100-count:*

| Group of cards | Running count |
|---|---|
| (10, 7) | -1 |
| (10, 5) | +1 |
| (A, 4) | 0 |
| (10, 10) | -5 |
| (10, 9, 5) | 0 |

| | |
|---|---|
| (10, A, 5) | -2 |
| (10, A, 7) | -4 |
| (10, 10, A) | -8 |
| (10, 10, 5, 7) | 0 |
| (10, 10, 4, 4) | +1 |
| (10, 10, 10, 5) | -4 |
| (10, 10, 10, 7) | -6 |
| (10, 10, 4, 2), (10, 10, 4, 3), (10, 10, 4, 6) | 0 |
| (10, 10, 2, 2), (10, 10, 2, 3), (10, 10, 2, 6), etc. | -1 |

## REMARKS CONCERNING ADJUSTED COUNTS

Assume that a player who uses the main-count system decides to improve the betting strategy by correcting for 5s and aces. For this, he should keep track of the running count FA (see adjusted counts, Chapter 3). He can do this mentally. In fact this is the method we recommend. Nevertheless, we observe that certain "material aids" can be used for following additional parameters. For example, the player may keep track of FA by using his left hand (see Fig. 1): At the beginning of the deal he should place his left thumb in the position indicated by 0, and he should leave it there, as long as FA = 0. If FA becomes +1, he should move the thumb in the position indicated by +1. If FA becomes +2, he should move the thumb in the

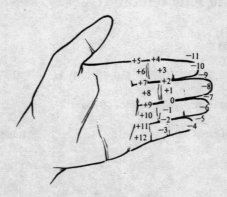

Figure 1

position indicated by +2. If FA becomes +1 again, he should move the thumb back in the position indicated by +1. Proceeding this way the player can keep track of FA as long as it remains between -11 and +12. We observe that only rarely will FA become smaller than -11, or greater than +12.

A variant of this method can be used to keep track of the number of unseen aces, in actual blackjack games.

Although we do not recommend the use of "material aids" for keeping track of additional parameters, other authors do.

## GENERAL REMARKS

We want to impress upon the reader that one should be able to make immediate decisions during actual play. The player who has to stop and think how to calculate the running index will, undoubtedly, have difficulties remembering the running counts corresponding to the parameters he is trying to follow. All the details should be clarified before one starts playing. One should not be requested to think unnecessarily so that one can think better when necessary.

I have been often asked – even by persons who should know better – whether one can keep track of various parameters, compute running indices and, at the same time, make strategic decisions. Particularly, can this be done in a casino, where so many things tend to divert the player's attention? The answer to this question is yes, it can be done, if one practices enough. The player who does not want to practice should not expect to win in casinos.

It is somewhat annoying to hear various persons complaining how difficult it is to learn to play blackjack well. Consider, for example, the game of tennis. It takes at least 6 months of sustained effort to learn to control the ball well enough, so that some pleasure can be derived from the game. Also, most "future tennis players" pay outrageous fees to some tennis coaches who only rarely are any good. Why should one expect that mastering a winning blackjack strategy – which might bring substantial profits to the player – require less effort than learning how to play a fair game of tennis?

# Bibliography

1. I. Anderson, *Turning the Tables in Las Vegas,* Vantage Books, New York, (1976).
2. J. Archer, *The Archer Method of Winning at 21,* Henry Regnery Co., Chicago, (1973).
3. H. Asbury, *The Sucker's Progress (An Informal History of Gambling in America from the Colonies to Canfield),* Dodd, Mead & Co., New York, (1938).
4. R. Baldwin, W. Cantey, H. Maisel and J. McDermott, "The Optimum Strategy in Blackjack," *Journal of the American Statistical Association,* 51, 429–439, (1956).
5. R. Baldwin, W. Cantey, H. Maisel, and J. McDermott, *Playing Blackjack to Win. A New Strategy for the Game of 21,* M. Barrows & Co. Inc., New York, (1957).
6. J. Braun, *The Development and Analysis of Winning Strategies for the Casino Game of Blackjack,* Chicago, Illinois, (1975).
7. J. Braun, *How to Play Winning Blackjack,* Data House Publishing Co., Inc., Chicago, Illinois, (1980).
8. R. A. Canfield, *Blackjack, Your Way to Riches,* Lyle Stuart, Secaucus, New Jersey, (1979).
9. C. R. Chamblis and T. C. Roginski, *Playing Blackjack in Atlantic City,* The GBC Press, Las Vegas, Nevada, (1981).
10. W. R. Eadington, *Gambling and Society,* Charles Thomas Publishing Co., Springfield, Illinois, (1976).
11. C. Edwards, *Perfecting Your Card Memory,* The GBC Press, Las Vegas, Nevada, (1974).
12. C. Einstein, *How to Win at Blackjack,* The GBC Press, Las Vegas, Nevada, (1975).
13. R. A. Epstein, *The Theory of Gambling and Statistical Logic,* Academic Press, New York, (1977).
14. S. W. Erdnase, *The Expert at the Card Table,* The GBC Press, Las Vegas, Nevada, (1975) (Reprint of the original 1902 edition).
15. B. P. Fabricand, *The Science of Winning,* Van Nostrand Reinhold Co., New York, (1980).
16. L. Fraikin, *Inside Nevada Gambling,* Exposition Press, New York, (1962).

17. B. Friedman, *Casino Games*, Golden Press, New York, (1973).

18. F. Garcia and G. Schindler, *Magic With Cards*, Reiss Games Inc., New York, (1975).

19. V. L. Graham and C. Ionescu Tulcea, *Three Parameter Blackjack Winning Strategy*, (2nd ed.), Evanston, Illinois, (1977).

20. V. L. Graham and C. Ionescu Tulcea, *A Book on Casino Gambling*, (2nd ed.), Van Nostrand Reinhold Co., New York, (1978).

21. P. A. Griffin, "The Rate of Gain in Player Expectation for Card Games Characterized by Sampling Without Replacement and an Evaluation of Card Counting Systems," in *Gambling and Society*, Charles Thomas Publishing Co., Springfield, Illinois, (1976), pp. 429–442.

22. P. A. Griffin, *On the Likely Consequences of Errors in Card Counting Systems*, Mathematics Department, Sacramento State University, Sacramento, California, (1976).

23. P. A. Griffin, *The Theory of Blackjack*, The GBC Press, Las Vegas, Nevada, (1979). Second expanded edition (1981).

24. D. Heath, *Algorithm for Computations of Blackjack Strategies*, Second Conference on Gambling, sponsored by the University of Nevada, Reno, (1975).

25. R. L. Holder and F. Downtown, "Casino Pontoon," *Journal of the Royal Statistical Society*, 135, 3, 222–224, (1972).

26. D. Huff, *How to Lie With Statistics*, W. W. Norton and Company, Inc., New York, (1954).

27. L. Humble and C. Cooper, *The Worlds Greatest Blackjack Book*, Doubleday and Co., Inc., New York, (1980).

28. C. Ionescu Tulcea, *Betting Systems I*, Technical Report, Northwestern University, (1979).

29. C. Ionescu Tulcea, *A Book on Casino Craps, Other Dice Games and Gambling Systems*, Van Nostrand Reinhold Co., New York, (1981).

30. K. Itá, *Counting Methods to Beat* 21, The GBC Press, Las Vegas, Nevada, (1976).

31. H. C. Levinson, *Chance, Luck and Statistics*, Dover Publications, Inc., New York, (1963).

32. M. MacDougall, *MacDougall – On Dice and Cards*, Coward-McCann Inc., New York, (1944).

33. A. R. Manson, A. J. Barr, and J. H. Goodnight, "Optimum Zero-Memory Strategy and Exact Probabilities for Four-Deck Blackjack," *The American Statistician*, 29, 2, 84–88, (1975).

34. E. McGuire, *The Phantom of the Card Table*, The GBC Press, Las Vegas, Nevada, (1976).

35. M. Newman, *Dealer's Special*, The GBC Press, Las Vegas, Nevada, (1979).

36. J. Noir, *Casino Holiday*, Oxford Street Press, Berkeley, California, (1968).

37. Ed Reid and O. Demaris, *The Green Felt Jungle*, Pocket Books Inc., New York, (1964).

38. L. Revere, *Playing Blackjack as a Business,* Lyle Stuart, Inc., New York, (1973).

39. L. Revere, *The Revere Advanced Point Count Strategy,* Paul Mann Publishing Co., Las Vegas, Nevada, (1973).

40. S. Roberts, *Winning Blackjack,* Scientific Research Services, Hollywood, California, (1979).

41. J. Scarne, *Scarne's Guide to Gambling,* Simon and Shuster, New York, (1978).

42. H. S. Smith, *I Want to Quit Winners,* Prentice Hall, Englewood Cliffs, New Jersey, (1961).

43. E. O. Thorp, "Favorable strategy for Twenty-one," *Proceedings of the National Academy of Sciences,* 47, 1, 110–112, (1961).

44. E. O. Thorp, *Beat the Dealer,* (2nd ed.), Random House, New York, (1966).

45. E. O. Thorp, "Optimal Gambling Systems for Favorable Games," *Review of the International Statistical Institute,* 37, 273–293, (1969).

46. E. O. Thorp and W. Walden, "The Fundamental Theorem of Card Counting, *International Journal of Game Theory,* 2, 2, (1973).

47. K. Uston, *Two Books on Blackjack,* Published by the author, Box 2121, Wheaton, Maryland 20902, (1979).

48. K. Uston, *Million Dollar Blackjack,* SRS Enterprises Inc., Hollywood, California, (1981).

49. W. Walden, *Solution of Games by Computation,* Ph. D. Thesis, New Mexico State University, (1964).

50. A. N. Wilson, *The Casino Gambler's Guide,* Harper and Row, New York, (1965).

51. S. Wong, *Professional Blackjack,* The Pi Yee Press, La Jolla, California, (1980).

52. B. D. Woon, *The Why, How and Where of Gambling in Nevada,* Bonanza Publishing Co., Reno, Nevada, (1953).

# Index

# INFORMATION IS POWER

With these almanacs, compendiums, encyclopedias, and dictionaries at your fingertips, you'll always be in the know. Pocket Books has a complete list of essential reference volumes.